What You Fear Is Who You Are

The Role of Fear in Relationships

David Thompson, Ph.D.
and
Krysten Thompson

MTR Corp.
Chicago, Illinois

What You Fear Is Who You Are
The Role of Fear in Relationships

Published by MTR Corp.

For information:
MTR Corp.
P.O. Box 10128
Chicago, Illinois 60610
www.whatyoufear.com

ISBN: 0-9705185-0-1

Printed in the United States of America

To Nancie, For Being The Dream

Contents

Chapter Seven

Chapter Eight

Chapter Nine

Chapter Ten

Part II

Evaluating Other People and Their Influence on Us

Chapter Eleven

Chapter Twelve

Chapter Thirteen

Chapter Fourteen

Introduction

"Nothing is so much to be feared as fear."

Henry David Thoreau

"O friend, never strike sail to a fear! Come into port greatly, or sail with God the seas."

Ralph Waldo Emerson

Chapter One

Confronting the Demons

Perhaps something was missing, something she hadn't seen, something beyond her analytical skills. Karen sat alone, oblivious to the tears coursing down her cheeks. She was considering suicide and had the means to do it. It was a thought that would have amazed her friends had they any inkling. This was not, however, an infrequent consideration on her part, and never more intensely felt than now.

What had she done wrong? This question seemed to be with her always, she thought, perhaps because she was raised by rather critical, cold, emotionally barren parents. But her parents hadn't been part of her life for years.

The question surfaced frequently during her too many sessions of therapy. At least therapy had brought occasional "answers," some insights into the causes of her self-doubts, even though little substantive change or progress was achieved.

God knows, her lack of success did not reflect a lack of effort. And she had learned many secrets about herself, including how often she tried to "avoid" reality. But now she was closer than ever to the ultimate avoidance, the conclusion that death was perhaps the only possible escape from her pain. For she knew that her greatest pain came from having to live with the inadequacies of the one person she disliked most, but could never get away from—herself.

The insights of therapy had shown Karen that her fear of being criticized drove her to be the perfect wife, that her fear of being seen as a failure led her to become the perfect mother, and her fear of being alone made her the perfect and willing friend of too many destructive people. Therapy had enabled Karen to see that her fear of being disliked clearly had led her to be the perfect employee, and that her fear of confrontations and of being disliked made her a perfect target for the selfish needs of others.

But Karen also realized that these insights had little effect on the fact that her husband had divorced her, that her children showed little interest in her, and that those destructive people seemed to be her only real "friends." Karen was conscious of the fact that her boss took advantage of her and that her friends, while "liking" her, had little real respect for her.

Caring people frequently told Karen what she must do: "You have to learn to respect yourself!" But no one told her how to achieve that lofty goal. Did people really think she didn't want to respect herself? Did people really feel that she enjoyed her depressing self-deprecation? Did people really think she enjoyed wallowing in fear?

Karen had to admit that even her years of therapy had probably helped erode her self-respect. Yet she found it too difficult to stop seeing Dr. Lattimore. He had become a good friend, a person who would listen and accept her without judgment. He was her safe harbor. But Dr. Lattimore seemed to feel successful when he had determined the fears in Karen that drove her to self-destructive behaviors. Those "successes" may have lessened *his* fears, but seemed to have little real long-term effect on Karen.

* * *

Karen reluctantly decided that she would make one last attempt to alleviate her own fears with as much effectiveness as she apparently lessened the anxieties and frustrations of others. And she knew the answers would have to come from herself. Therapy had at least taught her that too many people in her inner circle liked her fear-ridden state and the control it gave them over her. Worse, too many seemed uninterested, even uncomfortable, when Karen expressed her enthusiasm about life, rare though those feelings were.

As Karen softly wiped her tears, she concluded that her goal—her "Holy Grail"—would be to find the steps necessary to at least lessen one of the most damaging forces in her life, her fear. If she failed, then she knew the life left to her would not be worth living.

* * *

It is the thesis of this book that most inappropriate behavior—behavior that makes us feel inadequate, behavior that drives good people away from us—is driven by fear. And if we understand fear, we will better understand why we do what we do. Time doesn't necessarily heal all things. But understanding can take us a long way in that direction. And with this greater understanding should come more tolerance and sympathy, more patience, and less negative emotion, toward others and ourselves. More important, with this understanding should come more confidence on our part…with people and within ourselves.

Understanding fear should allow us to learn why we react ineffectively to people, why we say and do things we should not have said or done, and why we did not say and do the things we know we should have. Most important, through understanding fear, we can better know what to do when people make us uncomfortable, when they increase our fears.

So let's confront fear with our greatest asset—our mind. And through this confrontation we may well lessen our own anger, our bewilderment, our frustration and intolerance, our own fear and angry behavior toward others and ourselves. Then we may well become more patient, tolerant, sympathetic, and a good friend to those we should like and love, and confident enough to leave those who should not be a part of our life. With a greater understanding of fear, we should find ourselves enjoying life with greater confidence, increased calmness, and deeper happiness.

Fear

Just what is fear? Fear is an emotion we often feel when we think some *future* event might occur, an event we wouldn't like. The really pervasive fears of our lives are generally a reaction to something that is not there, not present with us at the moment but something that we anticipate might happen.

Excluding neurotic fears (heights or snakes), there are two basic things we fear in life: 1) people engaging in certain behaviors we find threatening (such as criticism or rejection) and 2) people *not* doing certain things we desperately want them to do (asking us on a date or proposing to us).

Almost all of our fears center on other people and what they might or might not do.

Our Responsibility

Most of us realize early in life that our own behavior can influence the behavior of other people and their behavior can influence our feelings, attitudes, and behavior. Cry and we get fed, clean up our room and we get a hug, talk back and we get yelled at (or worse), come in late and we get "grounded." So the behavior of others has a strong influence on making us who we are, especially in two areas:

* We usually make sure we're doing things that we believe will *prevent* people from behaving in ways we fear, e.g., if we fear criticism from abrasive persons, we may frequently act in a placating manner toward them.
* We also like to be sure we're not doing something that encourages behavior in others that we fear and want to *prevent*, e.g., criticizing someone whose anger we fear.

Fear=Excessive

But people might act in ways we don't want them to at **any** time. Thus, we must be on guard all the time we're interacting with them! So fear can easily become a most frequent and familiar companion. This has two crucial consequences.

1. If, for example, we fear the anger or rejection of others, we may often be subservient when we're with them. Indeed, because their anger or rejection could arise anytime, we may feel that we need to be subservient virtually all the time we're with them. Thus, our fear leads to excessive subservience on our part.

Our fear of someone doing something that scares us, therefore, leads us to engage in excessive behavior patterns, behaviors that are frequently inappropriate, e.g., occurring too often and too often at the wrong time.

2. This same fear of someone's anger or rejection may also lead us to assiduously avoid engaging in any aggressive behavior that might result in the dreaded anger, e.g., we never criticize or challenge anything they say or do. Thus, our fear leads us to excessive avoidance of certain behaviors.

Our fear of someone's doing something that frightens us also leads us to excessively avoid engaging in behavior that would be appropriate on occasion ("I wish I had said…").

People who are fearful of being criticized by others are often *excessively* passive or meek, believing that this helps to prevent others from criticizing them. But it should also be noted that they carefully avoid being aggressive. People who fear being rejected by a lover may frequently try to please them, thus avoiding the dreaded rejection; but they also excessively avoid doing anything that might displease them. People who fear intimacy are often excessively factual and emotionally barren; but they also adamantly avoid any discussion of personal feelings.

A shy person who dreads attention is often excessively quiet and withdrawn, avoiding at all cost any behaviors that might draw the attention of others. A person who fears being insignificant to others, on the other hand, often excessively seeks attention, too often interrupting and intruding, but also having great difficulty being a quiet listener. A person who fears lack of control is often excessively authoritative, demanding, and commanding, rarely engaging in any behavior that might be seen as needing others.

When people engage in extreme (excessive), inappropriate behavior, they are being driven by fear. When they excessively avoid engaging in behavior that is appropriate, they are being driven by fear.

What Best Describes a Person?

How can we best describe a person? The most accurate description of a person is their frequent, repetitive behavior. If a person is frequently and repetitively cheerful, but occasionally sad, we would still describe that person as cheerful. If someone is frequently, repetitively decisive, we describe them as decisive, even though once in a while they may be indecisive.

So frequent, repetitive behavior best describes a person. But what best meets the standard of frequent and repetitive? EXCESSIVE! If behavior is excessive, it's certainly frequent and repetitive! But if fear leads to excessive behavior and if excessive best meets the criterion of frequent and repetitive, then fear best describes a person!

One does not know a person, therefore, until one knows that person's fears. And knowing another person's fears will allow us to understand that person more completely than any other knowledge of them.

Are We Looking?

We see people in our inner circle a lot. But do we really know who they are? Most of us are so concerned with and driven by our own fears that we rarely take the time to think of others, even when they're part of our inner circle. This is an unfortunate mistake, one that leads to many frustrations.

Chris is a lovely woman, quite successful in a growing organization that prides itself on its aggressive, competitive and well-paid employees. As a regional sales manager, Chris has developed a highly competent team that gets results.

Her success in the business world, however, is matched by failure in her personal life. Chris is 38 years old, feels the biological clock ticking, and does not want to spend the rest of her life alone. Still, she has not been able to get a commitment from any of the men she felt were marriageable material.

Chris, unfortunately, is driven by a fear of failing (not a love of success). As a result, she is forceful and aggressive, but excessively so (fear=excessive). This leads to short-term success in the business world. She initially moved up the organization quickly, makes a good deal of money, has enormous prestige and ample power and influence.

In her personal life, however, her fear of failing has already led to disaster. In this area too, she is **excessively** forceful and aggressive. She moves fast and hard and expects the same of the men she dates. She is ready to commit quickly, almost impulsively. Chris has little time for "irrelevant nuances." She so quickly drives to a personal openness and frankness, and even intimacy, that she scares people. Her behavior, being extreme, borders on being tactless and controlling in the eyes of many.

Chris doesn't see any of this. Her fear of failure and of not achieving her goals stops her from seeing anything but the path to her target of marriage and eventually children.

As a result, Chris fails to see or even be aware of the fears of the men she dates. She does not see Mike's fear of being controlled, Jim's fear of being financially responsible for others, Al's fear of the unknown, Bill's fear of appearing inadequate (especially given Chris' financial success), Matt's fear of personal intimacy, Jack's fear of being ridiculed, Allen's fear of failure (especially in marriage, given his two previous divorces), Mike's fear of the possible boredom of always being with one woman, Rob's fear of being insignificant to a lot of other women if he marries one, Herb's fear of a woman's anger, etc., etc.

What is Chris' mistake? Being fearful of failing? Not necessarily. She wastes too much time on people who can't change, who lack confidence (the men in her life, who probably seek out her aggressive manner initially because they have their own fears to deal with). The big mistake is that Chris is so driven by her own fears that she can't focus on other people and who they are! But it's the fears of others that affect us, that lead to so many of our destructive relationships, frustrations, and even failures!

But Is Fear Sometimes Good?

Many people say some fear is good, it's a motivator that gives us an "edge." Baloney! Fear is always destructive in the long run because the specific behavior it drives always becomes excessive. Extremes of behavior are inappropriate rather than adaptive, rigid rather than flexible. This is why so few of us realize our potential and experience true happiness.

Excesses of behavior and the fears driving them prevent us from "seeing" our environment, from realizing who we're dealing with, what we can reasonably expect from others, and how they'll impact us over the long term.

This book is about changing this trap. It's about recognizing who the people in our inner circle are and why they do what they do, especially to us. It's also about recognizing who we are and what drives us to do what we do.

There is a tremendous freedom to be found by ridding ourselves of the fears that drive us. This freedom will lead to a calm, contented confidence. (With this confidence, we'll rid ourselves of the frustrations involved in not being able to confront those things and people we should confront.) More importantly, we'll develop the confidence and skills to seek and find those things, people, and constructive personal relationships that allow us enjoy a richer, more stimulating life.

The goal of *What You Fear Is Who You Are* is not only to give readers the insights to face and accept reality and the people around them as they are, but to also give readers the confidence to take the appropriate actions based on those insights. *What You Fear Is Who You Are* should help readers define and develop for themselves a world of good friends and lovers, a world of successful personal relationships that result in mutual confidence, love, and happiness.

Part I

Evaluating Ourselves

The man who fears suffering is already suffering from what he fears.

Michael de Montaigne

If a man harbors any sort of fear, it percolates through all his thinking, damages his personality, makes him landlord to a ghost.

Lloyd Douglas

Chapter Two

We Are Who We Are Not

Before we develop a plan to decrease our fears, we would do well to first find out what our fears are. Only then will we be able to focus on the right areas, do the right things, and make the right decisions that help us become more confident.

But No One Knows How Fearful I Am

We might bear in mind that fears are really quite common in people, more so than is readily apparent. The strongest of us is frequently driven by fear. If a person is confident (lacks fear) in twenty areas, but is fearful in one, that one will tend to dominate many of their thoughts and actions. If, for example, a man is confident in many situations but excessively "macho," it's because he's driven by a fear of being seen as frightened by other people. This fear will tend to drive much of his thinking and behavior when he is dealing with people, which is most of the time.

When we label people as confident and are awed by their "strength," we are often responding to the fact that they don't fear the same things we fear. Even the "macho" fellow will sometimes be impressed by the "confident" individual who can freely admit to being frightened on occasion. How frequently (and naively) we see others as so confident, especially in relation to ourselves, is startling. And though we rarely know it, because no one says anything, these "confident" people often feel the same way about us. Why? Because they don't see us as fearing the things in others they fear.

Know Thyself

We'll only know ourselves when we know our fears.

But what are our fears? Fear leads to excesses in behavior. To know our own fears then, all we have to do is note our excesses and determine why we engage in them. But this generally won't work. Why?

Because our excesses in behavior won't be seen as excessive by us! Others may see them as extreme, but too often we'll see that as their problem, as being just another sign of their criticalness, hostility, or poor judgment. After all, if we truly saw our behavior as inappropriate in a given area, we probably wouldn't behave in that manner.

What We Have Difficulty Doing

Mary is excessively placating and subservient in order to prevent people from being **angry** with her. And she is best described as "placating and subservient." But Mary probably would not see it that way. She would be likely to describe herself as "cooperative and not wanting to hurt anyone; I'm just trying to be civil." And so would most of us "justify" our extreme, fear-driven behavior, thereby gaining little self-insight. So we must have a better way than "excessiveness" of determining what fears truly do drive *us*.

Mary also learned long ago that criticizing someone increases the likelihood that people will be angry with her. (People have yelled at Mary because they were angry with her when she criticized them.) As a result, the behavior of criticizing others has been "punished out" of Mary. She now finds it emotionally difficult to criticize anyone so she just can't do it.

Mary should be able to criticize others when they deserve it. She may have an abusive boyfriend or a bad boss who richly deserve her criticism. Criticizing them may be the best thing she could do for herself and them. But she cannot bring herself to criticize them. Berating her for her weakness and/or arguing with her rationally about it proves futile for everyone.

Because we like Mary so much, we may be incredulous (and angry) at her and her inability to criticize people who are so unfair to her. We want her to at least stand her ground with her abusive boyfriend or obnoxious boss. But our frustration with her results from the fact that we don't have her fear of standing up to "bad" people. People who share her fear of people's anger will be much more tolerant and understanding of her behavior.

How Did We Get This Way?

Mary learned to not criticize anyone at an early age. She criticized her father and got spanked. She criticized her mother and was sent to her room without dinner. They were not tolerant parents. She criticized her older brother and he physically made sure she never did again. Mary is now 35 years old. If she criticized someone (especially a confident person), most likely nothing would happen to her. Certainly no one will spank her or send her to her room or beat her up. **But Mary will never know this. Why? Because she won't criticize anyone!**

In sum, if we want to "know" Mary, it's important to realize that she is excessively meek and placating and she is best described that way. Mary fears the anger of others, and that is also important to know.

But because she fears someone's anger, she is also fearful of criticizing anyone and cannot do it. And this, too, is important to know. We would do well also to consider the behavior Mary cannot engage in. For this is also who Mary is.

Who Mary Is And Is Not

At an early age, Mary criticizes several family members:

Their reaction: Father spanks her.

Mother sends her to her room.

Brother "beats her up."

Effect on Mary: Mary learns to fear people's anger.

Mary learns not to criticize people.

Mary learns to become placating and subservient.

Most of her friends would now agree that Mary is a "placating, subservient" person who fears the anger of others. But just as important, Mary's response repertoire—the behavior she has at her command, what she feels comfortable doing with people—is narrowed. (The broader the gene pool of a species, the more adaptive the species; similarly, the broader our response repertoire, the more adaptive we can be.) Mary cannot criticize people even when it is appropriate, productive, and beneficial to all involved. Just as her excessive placating behavior is driven by fear, so also is her excessively avoided "criticizing" behavior.

So, like Mary, we are what we are not, what we cannot be, what we feel uncomfortable doing with people. We can be described in terms of our frequent, repetitive, even inappropriate behavior patterns. But we can also be described in terms of what we cannot do, what we feel uncomfortable doing, what ways we have difficulty behaving with others. If we are to lessen our own fears, this is extremely important to know.

What Drives a Person, a Love of the Good or a Fear of the Bad?

Fear drives much of our behavior. If we have difficulty acknowledging fear and its crucial role in our life, we may have a troubled, frustrating life indeed. For fear not only leads us to avoid certain behaviors, but also certain people. Then we end up criticizing our poor choice of friends when we should be looking at those we avoid because of our own anxieties.

*She likes and seeks out men who are dependent on her? Maybe not. Maybe she only dates dependent men because she fears men who aren't dependent on her.

*She likes and seeks out men who fear intimacy? Maybe not. Maybe she is relaxed with "macho" men because she fears men who are comfortable with intimacy.

*She likes and seeks out depressed men? Maybe not. Maybe she surrounds herself with depressed men because she fears and avoids happy men.

*She likes people who are bad for her? Maybe not. Maybe she's always with bad people because she fears people who are good for her.

Why Is What We Cannot Do Important?

There are three reasons that our inability to behave in certain ways is important.

1. Our Competence and Confidence

First, it means that our response repertoire is narrowed. Thus, we're less effective with people and too often more critical of ourselves for being unable to do and say those things we know we should do and say.

Almost all behavior is appropriate at one time or another. People who are *always indecisive* are driven by fear. They may fear being decisive and criticized for their decisions. Those who are *always decisive* are also driven by fear. They may well fear being indecisive and seen as weak or dependent by others. The confident person is mostly decisive, but is sometimes indecisive. It is appropriate to say "I don't know" at times, and the person who cannot is fearful.

People who are *always dependent* are driven by fear. They fear relying on themselves, doing things on their own. But those who are *always independent* are also driven by fear. They fear being seen as needing others. Both the *always* dependent and the *always* independent person have narrow response repertoires. The confident person is mostly independent, but is able to say occasionally, "Can you help me with this?" The confident person has a wider response repertoire and is thus able to adapt better to most situations.

When we find it too difficult to engage in a behavior that would have been appropriate for the occasion ("I should have said..."), that behavior was probably punished out of us. The fear of engaging in the behavior is the result of our anticipating the person's reaction to it. This made us more narrow in our repertoire and made us less effective in our dealings with people.

John is too dependent. He always seeks out the views of others and never makes a decision until he knows which way everyone else is going. John is driven by fear. Cheryl is too independent. She never seeks out the advice of others, rarely admits not knowing something, and won't let anyone do anything for her. Cheryl, despite her "tough" facade, is driven by fear. (She probably fears being controlled or seen as "needing" someone.)

A confident person cannot be described in one way or another. They are different beings at different times with different people. This is not hypocrisy. This reflects a good sensitivity to the differences in those around us and an effectiveness in responding appropriately to our always changing environment.

So a competent, confident person has a wide response repertoire from which to draw in order to respond effectively to the many different people and different situations encountered daily. One of the goals of this book will be to help readers increase their response repertoire.

2. What Is Out of Sight Must Be in Our Mind

Focusing on what a person cannot do is sometimes much more beneficial in lessening their fear than focusing on what they do excessively.

Too often, however, we become caught up with their "bad" (irrational) behavior because that's what we see, that's what impacts us.

We may focus on the sadness of our constantly depressed friend, for example, because that's the behavior we see, the behavior that affects and often frustrates us. We might do better to focus on their *fear of being happy.* We may focus too often on the complaining of our negative friend because our friend subjects us to their irritating bitterness so often. If we want to change our negative friends, however, we might do better focusing on their *fear of showing enthusiasm.* Can they overcome their excessively negative orientation if they don't overcome their fear of being enthusiastic and positive? Doubtful.

Can we overcome our immoderate "attraction" to bad people in our lives if we don't address our excessive avoidance (fear) of good people? Probably not (especially if we feel that the only alternative to bad people is being alone). Should we continue to punish the frequent and frustrating indecisiveness of our significant other or address their fear of being decisive?

Observing excessive behaviors is the best tool for evaluating someone else. Focusing on their excessively avoided behavior, however, is often the best way to lessen their fear.

3. Truly Knowing Thyself

The third reason we want to focus on which behaviors are excessively avoided is that it is the best way to identify our own fears.

The easiest way to discover someone else's fears is to note what behaviors they engage in excessively. But our own excesses in behavior are not excessive to us. Too often, we'll deny and ignore suggestions that we're behaving in a "childish and immature manner." Any supposed example of extreme behavior on our part is easily "justified" in our minds by the circumstances and/or people who brought about the behavior. ("The reason I seemed indecisive with Jim is that he's always so critical; whenever I make a decision, he automatically says it's wrong.").

So the fears of others can best be discovered by noting their excesses in behavior. Our fears can best be determined by noting which reasonable behaviors we excessively avoid.

And that is just what this book is intended to do. There are certain behaviors *everyone* should be able to engage in at the appropriate time, especially with someone *important in their life.* Our inability to do so, our discomfort with certain patterns of behavior, should tell us where our fears rest.

In the next eight chapters will be listed 16 common behaviors that everyone should be able to engage in periodically with someone important in their life and/or with their significant other. Readers will be asked to engage in these behaviors. Hesitation over doing so will tell us what is probably feared from people in our inner circle.

Summary

1. The *excessive* behaviors of a person are usually apparent to others and are the best way to evaluate someone else.

2. Being subjected to the excesses in behavior of those in our inner circle is often frustrating to us. It is this behavior in someone else that too often draws our attention and our punitive efforts to change them.

3. Early in our lives, we found that certain behaviors on our part led others to behave in ways we didn't like. Their behavior "punished" us and led us to feel uncomfortable behaving in those ways. The behaviors eliminated from our repertoire can range from being decisive to being indecisive, from being dependent to being independent, from being aggressive to being passive, from being happy to being sad, from seeking out to avoiding people who are good for us.

4. A narrow range of behaviors in our repertoire makes us less adaptable, hence less effective with people. The inability to engage in "normal" behaviors too often increases our self-criticism and decreases our confidence.

5. The behaviors a person avoids engaging in are often as important to note as their excessive behaviors when trying to lessen their fear. It is frequently difficult to lessen extreme or irrational behavior unless the behavior being avoided is addressed.

6. Focusing on behavior people **avoid** would allow us to *reinforce* "tendencies" on their part to try to engage in these feared behaviors.

7. For self-analysis, we will first determine what reasonable people should be able to do when appropriate, especially with those who are important in their lives. Then, in the coming chapters, we'll focus on which of those behaviors **we** find it difficult to engage in with those who are important in our lives. This will help tell us what we truly fear in ourselves and others.

Chapter Three

Few of us have focused on what we are not, i.e., which behaviors we avoid. So let's list some behaviors most confident people have in their repertoire, ready to call forth when appropriate. By determining what types of behavior are difficult for us to engage in, we'll know what fears need to be considered and confronted.

Please remember, nobody's asking us to change our behavior (it's too difficult). *Our goal is greater self-insight.* And that insight will prove valuable. By knowing where our fears lie, we'll be especially sensitive to these same fears in our friends, those in our inner circle.

Why care about these fears in our friends? Because we so often pick as friends those with whom we have something in common—namely, our fears. That's what makes us feel comfortable with them; they're unlikely to bring up situations that embarrass us because of our common fears. But because we share the same fears, our friends are also unlikely to help us overcome them. A person fearful in a given area has little desire to lessen the fear of someone else in that area.

Self-Assessment

In the chapters that follow, we will determine which of the following sixteen behaviors we have difficulty engaging in, especially with our significant other. We will try them out, if not with our significant other, at least with someone who is quite important to us, maybe even our boss. (The more important someone is to us, the more fear we frequently feel with them.) If we hesitate in any area, we may well have determined a specific fear in ourselves.

1. Fear of Criticism

Can we readily and easily ask of a significant other:
"What's my greatest shortcoming?"
If we are fearful of doing this, maybe it's because we have a **fear of being criticized.**

Some Causes

The fear of being criticized is probably the most pervasive fear in our society. As we shall see, anything associated with a negative becomes negative to us. Criticism has probably been associated with just about every other negative in "the book." From being sent to bed early to being embarrassed in front of our classmates for a poor test result, almost all negatives are preceded or accompanied by criticism. Criticism is an important part of most confrontations, arguments, rejections, expressions of dislike, refusals of a raise or promotion, and so forth.

Timing

But asking people to tell us "our greatest shortcoming" must be done at the right time. And that is **not** when people are angry at us and are more than happy to tell us about our greatest shortcoming. For then the feedback will be intended to hurt; it will lead to more problems than it solves.

The time to ask people about our greatest shortcoming is when everything is going well, when frustrations and angers are at a minimum. This increases the likelihood that the feedback we get will be constructive, meaningful, and helpful for everyone. Some will be hesitant to answer our question. But if we ask them in a gentle, informal manner and at the right time, most people will respond constructively.

Some Consequences

The behaviors most of us engage in with the goal of preventing criticism from others are legion. Fear of criticism is a fear that must always be checked within ourselves, with almost everyone with whom we interact on a daily basis. To this end, from time to time we would do well to ask people we see frequently what they consider our greatest shortcoming.

This will provide a number of benefits, three of which we'll discuss now:

1. Our fears give other people a good deal of control over us. Deliberately and frequently seeking critical feedback from others will help "desensitize" us to being criticized. If we're less sensitive to criticism, others will have much less ability to control us in a destructive way. That is, not being so sensitive to criticism will make us less concerned with what others think of us, especially in "potentially" negative situations (fear is pervasive because so many situations are "potentially" negative).

2. Actively seeking criticism will help prevent "surprises" in relationships. Friends in our inner circle, especially our significant other, will often hesitate to criticize us, even when they're hurt and angry with us. This can cause their frustrations and angers to fester and grow to unmanageable proportions without our knowledge. Then, when the "dam breaks," we wind up in overly intense confrontations (far out of proportion to the event that broke the dam). Then we're bewildered and confused and become angry ourselves.

By seeking out criticism regularly, we give people an opportunity to express themselves and their frustrations before they have developed to an overly strong intensity. We're able to "nip problem areas in the bud" by defusing negative situations before they get out of hand and lead the relationship to spiral downward, sometimes quickly and uncontrollably.

3. Actively eliciting feedback can give us valuable information about who we are and how people see us. The alternative is to live in a vacuum. This is a sure way to encourage misunderstanding and petty bickering over things of minor importance. Many arguments are a

smokescreen that allow everyone to avoid addressing the real problem: who we are.

Importance of the Fear of Being Criticized

The *fear* of being criticized (as opposed to actually being criticized) is so important that it should be confronted in ourselves or others before any other fears or problems are addressed. Confronting negative issues with someone in our inner circle is often painful and almost always involves criticism of some sort. Then on these occasions,we or they are being hit with two barrels: the negative issue itself that is being confronted and the criticism implicit in bringing up the negative issue in the first place.

When, for example, someone's fear of intimacy is confronted, the confrontation will almost always involve criticizing that person. If the person is overly sensitive to criticism, they'll be hurt on two fronts: by the attack on their fear of intimacy, and the triggering of their fear of criticism by the implicit criticism involved. This will be too much for most people to handle, and they'll become defensive at best or will counterattack at worst.

In sum, if we or someone we love has shortcomings, we must address those shortcomings. The alternative is to have the shortcomings express themselves at different times and continually affect the relationship in destructive ways. If our significant others are too frequently negative and critical, for example, that is the behavior we should address. They may continually criticize restaurants, movies, people, and so forth. Arguing with them each time they do is both futile and destructive. Their behavior of being critical and fearful of being positive and enthusiastic must be addressed if real change is to occur.

But addressing any shortcoming will almost always involve criticism of some kind. If the person with the shortcoming is overly fearful of criticism, addressing the shortcoming is the same as confronting two fears at the same time, the fear motivating the shortcoming and the fear of criticism. The result is almost certain to be resistance.

The fear of being criticized must not be excessive, or must be lessened, before *any* other negative issues, shortcomings, or fears are approached.

Sources of Feedback

We have found that fear leads people to engage in some behaviors excessively and to excessively avoid engaging in others. In the case of criticism, aggressive people who fear being criticized are often excessively critical of others. Be it a boss or spouse, highly critical people have found the best defense is an offense. Most people hesitate to criticize them because they fear a counterattack. The passive person who fears criticism, on the other hand, will assiduously avoid criticizing anyone.

Both aggressive and passive persons who fear being criticized are usually successful in preventing it; the former by attacking, the latter by withdrawing. Frequent constructive feedback is essential for everyone. Aggressive or passive persons who have a deep fear of being criticized, therefore, are not good sources of *constructive* feedback. This is one reason that anyone who shares our fear (our friends) is usually not effective in helping us lessen that fear.

"What is my greatest shortcoming?" is a crucial question, one we should frequently ask those in our inner circle. It's a question that must readily and spontaneously trip forth. It tells people we want to grow, we want feedback, we seek their input. Over the long term, it tells people we're confident enough to seek critical feedback, thus their threats of criticizing us will have little impact.

"What is my greatest shortcoming?" tells the important people in our lives (spouses, significant others, friends, bosses, subordinates, colleagues) that we value their opinion, we'll listen to them, we respect them. It helps our interactions with people in our inner circle to become more open and spontaneous, more cooperative and communicative,

more relevant. Feedback from significant others in our lives tells us who they are, what they want from us, how they will try to influence us to change if they are to be happy in the relationship. That will tell us whether they're good for us. Most important, seeking criticism can give us invaluable feedback about who we are, what we should concentrate on to develop ourselves, and who we need around us to do so.

2. Fear of Rejection

Turning again to "normal" behavior, we must ask ourselves if we have difficulty telling our significant others: "If you can't stop doing that, maybe we shouldn't continue seeing each other."

Maybe they do treat us badly (even though we exaggerate their assets and minimize their liabilities to our friends). But, we won't confront them with their obvious problems and unrealistic demands. Why? Maybe we **fear rejection.**

But doesn't the above comment reflect a fear of rejecting someone else, not a fear of being rejected? True, but if we fear rejection from people, we often fear rejecting people—it might get us what we fear, being rejected in turn. We are so intent on preventing some behavior in others that we don't want to trigger it in them by engaging in it ourselves. As we've seen, if we fear criticism, we often avoid criticizing someone else: They may retaliate and criticize us back.

That's why we seek out as friends people who share our fears; having fears like ours means they're less likely to engage in the behaviors we fear (like criticizing or rejecting us), so we feel comfortable around them.

Some Causes

People who fear rejection often have been raised by cold, distant, and emotionally withdrawn parents who frequently used rejection as a controlling tool ("Go to your room; you can't go out and play with your friends.") This often leads children to become too dependent on the acceptance of others as the criterion by which they judge their own self worth. Not being invited to parties, on dates, and so forth, then becomes indicative of rejection, hence catastrophic.

Some Dire Consequences of the Fear of Rejection

A big problem exists with fear. The behaviors it drives a person to engage in have an incredible and ironic result: They actually get the person the very thing they fear when they're dealing with confident people. *Our fear increases the likelihood that confident people will behave toward us in the very way we're trying to prevent them from behaving.*

I start to date Marge and Sue. I fear they will reject and leave me. Since I'm fear-driven, my behavior will become excessive. My fear leads me to smother them. Marge is confident, Sue is not. Marge doesn't fear rejection, Sue does. Because of my fear-driven smothering (excessive) behavior, confident Marge rejects and leaves me. **My fear got me the very thing I feared…with a confident person.**

But fearful Sue loves my smothering. Indeed, she loves me the more for it. Sue and I develop a close relationship. After all, we have a lot in common—our mutual fears of rejection and the resulting love of smothering behavior by the other. Because Marge left me (my dreaded rejection), I grow suspicious of confident women! I seek out fearful women like Sue, with whom I feel comfortable. Our common fears lead us to be content (safe) being smothered by each other and, in turn, smothering each other. Thus we each reinforce the other's fear, dooming both of us to a continuation of this most destructive emotion.

We soon reach the point of being fearful if the other person doesn't smother us (call us every day). We smother and are smothered by our fear and those who share it with us.

And soon we'll be uncomfortable around—and learn to avoid—confident people (the ones who have the most constructive impact on us). Worse, we'll seek out fearful people, who have the worst

impact on us but with whom we feel comfortable. There are many reasons that fear is such a destructive, formidable enemy, and this is one of the biggest.

How many people, fearing rejection, refuse to be "vulnerable"? In so doing they refuse to tell significant others how much they like them, how nice they are, what a pleasure it is to be with them, how much they want to be with them, and how much they sometimes miss them.

They don't tell them these things because they fear being vulnerable. To what? Rejection. So they are seen as cold...and rejecting. So they get rejected (by confident people, anyway). How many of us have wanted to ask someone out, but feared rejection? What did we get in return for our fears? No date—but that is the very same result as if we had been rejected.

Do we suffer more because of our fear of rejection? Without question. But doesn't it hurt to have someone tell you, "I don't want to see you anymore"? Or, "I'm sorry. I really can't date you now." Of course. But does it hurt us to be always avoiding rejection? Does it hurt us to be constantly passive, placating, to be forever playing up to the whims, desires, and threats of someone who may not want us anyway? If we took the risk of eliciting rejection, we'd at least know where we stood with this person. And if confident, self-interested behavior on our part means rejection and ending up alone, so be it. We would probably end up in that position with people of this sort anyway.

We might try to think of the worst shortcoming of someone important in our lives or even of our significant other. Can we really continue to live with it, or will it be too destructive of us and our confidence? If the latter, let's confront them with it and the possibility of leaving them (rejection) if they continue that behavior toward us. We should be able to do this when it's reasonable to do so.

Is it too difficult to do? Then we know we have a problem that must be addressed. And we are better able to address it constructively if we know what it is.

Summary

The behaviors we have difficulty engaging in, especially with significant others, often tell us what *our* fears are. We should be able to:

1. Ask our significant others what they feel is our greatest shortcoming.

2. Tell our significant others that we should consider discontinuing the relationship if they repeatedly do something we know is destructive for us over the long term.

Chapter Four

3. Fear of Being Insignificant

Would the following statement be difficult to make to your significant other? "I think I need a little 'down time.'" "If you don't mind, I'd like to be alone for a while and just do some reading."

This is probably a difficult statement for some of us to make, especially to someone we want to like us. But it is an especially difficult response for those of us who **fear being insignificant** (unimportant) to others, especially those who are so important to us.

To want to be important/significant to someone is realistic. It leads us to behave constructively. To *fear* being unimportant/insignificant to someone is not realistic. This fear usually leads to excessive behaviors on our part and associates us with negatives to other people.

We're each driven by our own fears. And what people think of us is the source of many of our fears. So most of us have this in common: We want to influence others, if only to prevent them from behaving in a manner we fear. And if we're not important/significant to someone, we feel that our words and actions will be of little consequence to them.

How do we know we're significant to someone? Two of the most important signs are that they are emotionally responsive to us and that they "seek us out" by initiating intimate interactions with us.

Some Causes

The fear of being insignificant to people who are important in our lives usually develops when we are raised by parents who fear intimacy and are not emotionally responsive. Difficulties with intimacy and a lack of emotional responsiveness are usually more common among men than women. The fear of being insignificant in personal relationships is, consequently, more common among women than men. Seeking "normal" emotional responsiveness from a pervasively cold, indifferent father can have a lasting impact.

Many fathers, for example, are more comfortable with work and sports than with the emotional spontaneity of their children. Striving to elicit an emotional reaction from a father who fears intimacy can be a frustrating task indeed. And it's this kind of excessive striving for attention (emotional reactions) that best describes those of us who fear being insignificant.

Some Consequences

Smothering relationships are often based on the fear of being insignificant. Constant phone calls, interruptions, frequent time demands, long-winded discussions until the wee hours, overly strong emotional reactions to others—all often stem from an excessive need to alleviate one's own fear of being insignificant to other people.

What will alleviate a person's fear of being insignificant? An emotional reaction on our part directed toward them. Will the reinforcer help? Yes. But only in a transient, short-lived way, like all positive reinforcers (as we shall see).

> Mary: Jim, you're very important to me.
> Jim: Really? How do you mean?
> Mary: Well, I like being around you.
> Jim: Oh, that's great. I really like being around you too (Jim is now feeling good and is confident). We do have some good times together, don't we?
> Mary: Sure. Say, I've got to return that dress I bought the other day. You know, the pink and white one. The darn thing

doesn't fit me right. This is the second time that's happened. I'll see you later tonight.

Jim: Right. Say, what did you think of that shirt I bought the other day? (Because Mary is now focusing on something else, her dress, Jim's fear is returning and will soon drive his smothering behavior again.)

Mary: I liked it. Well, I'm going to return the dress now. I'll see you when I get back.

Jim: Hey, you know what, I wouldn't mind going over there with you. I'd like to see some of the stores in that mall. (Mary will soon wonder if she can ever get away from this guy, even for a little while.)

Fear often gets us what we fear, especially from confident people. Thus, the fear of being insignificant often gets us just that. If we truly fear being insignificant to others, we are often shunned, avoided, and fled from, especially by confident people who don't like being smothered.

Dangers of Being With a Partner Who Fears Being Insignificant

The *joy* of having a partner who fears being insignificant to us stems from their frequent concern for us and the fact that they are so ready to take care of us.

The *danger* of a partner who fears being insignificant to us is that they often don't want us to like ourselves! They don't like confidence in a significant other. They prefer dependency, a dependency that requires the "loved one" to rely on them for advice and guidance, a dependency that leads others to feel that they need them. And they achieve this ignoble goal by getting the loved one to dislike themself. How? By subtly criticizing them. Not open criticism. They might be rejected, and then they'd be insignificant.

How do they subtly criticize us? First, by frequently associating us with negatives, combining the criticism with a caring gesture ("You're really not doing that right; here, let me help you."). Second, by punishing our independence through criticism of any actions we take or decisions we make without having asked for their advice ("Why would you pay so much for this; I could have gotten it for you at a much better price.") Thus, we learn to be uncomfortable with ourselves and our judgment without their guidance.

Many parents, for example, frequently are critical of their grown children precisely because their children are grown! Their children have left the nest and have become too independent and self-sufficient. The adult children no longer need their parents. Feeling insignificant to their children, the parents fall back on the time when they were significant, when their children were concerned about their reactions, views, and responses. When was that? When the children were small, were dependent on them, and the parents readily told them what to do and what *not* to do (and just as readily punished them if they did it).

The result: Parents who are in frequent contact with their grown children, but who (excessively) criticize them. These criticisms, of course, usually turn their more confident children even further away from them. This leads to the parents' feeling more insignificant and becoming more critical. And this, in turn, leads to more withdrawal by confident children. Fear thus gets the parents the very thing they're trying to prevent. (Fearful children, of course, will feel inadequate and become more dependent on their parents.)

Is a significant other overly critical? Maybe it's because they fear being insignificant. And if we don't effectively and permanently lessen their fear of being insignificant to us, our confidence and respect for ourselves (our most precious asset) will drop quickly if we stay with them.

Excessively Avoided Behavior

Those who fear being insignificant usually have a strong need to control others, to make others dependent on them. Conversely, they also have a strong fear of others controlling them; they are much more inclined to give advice than take it. As a result, the person who fears being insignificant usually tries to prevent people from feeling that they are of any importance to them. Consider the individual who can't be on time, can't remember birthdays, forgets to bring gifts at appropriate times. Too often, we get angry when they do these things. But that is the very thing the person who fears being insignificant wants most from us: an emotional reaction. That's what proves to them they're significant to us. Being on time elicited no emotion from us. Being late elicits a strong emotional reaction.

Some people can't just sit quietly and listen to others, can't focus on others, and have no interest in what others are doing, have done, or will do. These people fear being insignificant to others, so excessively that they can't accept anyone else's being the center of attention. But they are really driven to prevent anyone else from feeling significant to them. Thus, they can't ask questions of others. They are seen as self-centered. They don't ask about your day. Why? Because the focus would swing to you—and away from them. They can't listen to others. When the conversation centers on them, they are wonderfully responsive and expressive, thus they are stimulating to be with. But when people talk about others, their responses are perfunctory, their attention wanders—until the topic of conversation settles again on them.

It is important to reemphasize that to *want* to be important to a particular person is fine. It leads to realistic, appropriate behavior that is flexible and adaptable to the environment. It leads us to do constructive things with that person, to appreciate their assets, to reinforce them, to love their confidence and respect of themselves. It leads us to focus on them, to care about their successes, their feelings and attitudes.

To *fear* not being important to a person is quite the opposite. It leads to rigid, excessive behaviors that are not adaptable to the environment but only to the individual's needs. It leads the individual to do destructive things with and to other people. It leads the individual to criticize the shortcomings of others, to punish their mistakes, to like and strengthen the other person's fears and poor image of themselves. And, because their destructive behavior is fear-driven, it is grossly inappropriate.

4. Fear of Being Seen as a Failure

Would you have difficulty saying the following to a significant other? "Man, did I botch that project up. I dropped so many balls at work today, they started calling me 'butter fingers.'"

Many people assiduously avoid any self-deprecating remarks. They cannot laugh at themselves. That's because they fear being looked down on by others; they fear **being seen as a failure.**

It is important to note that fear is centered on the behavior of others. Thus, it is not failing we fear; it's *being seen* as a failure by others—an important distinction. And it's the possibility of being seen as a failure by others that leads to the fear and the resulting excessive behavior patterns.

Some Causes

The fear of being seen as a failure is often a result of being raised by highly competitive parents who frequently compare their children's performance with that of others, usually superior others. This is done under the guise of motivating their children to "stretch." Children often come out unfavorably in these comparisons and quickly learn to fear being seen as a failure. These attitudes are often strengthened in the games children play, the "losers" frequently being taunted and ridiculed. This orientation, destructive as it may be, is rarely frowned on in a society as competitive as ours. (Many managers in business use contests to "motivate" their people, giving little thought to the fact that for every motivated winner, there may be many "demotivated," frustrated losers.)

* * *

Most of us want to impress people periodically with our physical prowess or beauty, our intellectual abilities, or our financial success. But most of us can also admit to a mistake or laugh at our blunders or our carelessness once in a while. Not the person who fears being seen as a failure!

* * *

Excessive Behaviors

He's a workaholic, has a driving need to prove himself, extols his successes accordingly, is intensely ambitious, and has little time for family and friends—except when he is intent on impressing them. He can't relax on weekends or vacations and sometimes gets terrible headaches when he's forced to go on them. He justifies all this on the basis of his responsibility to support his beloved family, the same family with whom he rarely spends time. He just wants to be financially "successful" for his family. Actually, this person doesn't want anything; he wants to *avoid* something. And that's the driving force in his life: being seen as a failure.

Fear of What?

"I just had to buy that Mercedes." Fear of being seen as a failure in the prestige and status area.

"I had a meeting the other day with several CEOs of Fortune 500 companies." Fear of being seen as a failure in the "power" area.

"Actually, I could bench-press quite a bit more than that if I hadn't hurt myself." Fear of being seen as a failure in the physical prowess area.

"He was the club champ, so I was a little surprised I could beat him so easily." Fear of being seen as a failure in the competitive "losing" area.

"I guess I come on too strong sometimes, because people seem to be intimidated by me rather easily." Fear of being seen as a failure in the "dominance" area.

"She was still another woman who wouldn't let go of me. She was almost stalking me." Fear of being seen as a failure in the "desirable" area.

"I really get tired of people needing me so much and always calling me." Fear of being seen as a failure in the "being needed and sought after" area.

Excessively Avoided Behavior

The intensely ambitious, hard-driving guy often marries the unambitious, "sweet," and usually quite attractive woman who is quite content being a homemaker. She not only doesn't try to impress, she self-deprecates and is quite readily impressed by others, just as readily and openly expressing her admiration for their successes. Indeed, when she did work, she turned down promotions, took jobs far below her capabilities, and always gave others credit for everything accomplished, even by her.

How could these two get together, let alone marry? What on earth do they have in common? The most important thing of all—their common fear of being seen as a failure. He does it with his aggressive need to impress others with his increased responsibilities. She does it by avoiding responsibility (and therefore the potential of failing and being seen as a failure). Who could possibly see and label her as a failure, even in raising her children, when she spends so much money on competent nannies, the best schools, the most organized (expensive) after-school activities? But she sees that responsibility always rests with others. Her fear of being seen as a failure causes her to avoid assuming any responsibility herself. She avoids competition. Indeed, that's why her fear-driven husband married her. His fear of being seen as a failure by others is not possible with her. No one can ever be a failure in her eyes; she is "sweet" indeed.

Unfortunately, this scenario often plays itself out in business. Because persons who are fearful of being seen as a failure drive themselves so hard, they usually attain high-level positions in an organization, often becoming CEOs. But they then surround themselves with weak people who present no competitive threat or would not see them as a failure, i.e., they surround themselves with frightened, incompetent people. Thus do some hard-driving, "successful" CEOs leave an organization bankrupt.

The fear of being seen as a failure leads them to focus on the image they create: Others see them arrive at work early and leave late; admire the pretty women they're with, and how well they dress; observe how appropriate the women's behavior is with others, and how well other people respond to them, hence to him. This person seeks out positive feedback only. Compliments and accolades alleviate his fear of being seen as a failure, even if only temporarily. Criticism is avoided at all costs. People who fear being seen as a failure frequently try to intimidate people so that criticism is kept to a minimum.

Some Consequences

Excessively extolling our virtues to others because of our fear of being seen as a failure often leads people to feel sorry for us, i.e., to see us as a failure. At least they think so when viewing our excessive attempts to impress others. As a result, people tend to avoid us when possible.

There are few things that will get people to be more comfortable with us than our occasional (not excessive) self-deprecation, our ability to laugh at ourselves. Working some self-deprecating response into a conversation can have an enormous rapport-building effect on a relationship. Why? Because it temporarily lessens the other person's fear of being criticized by us. And those who fear being looked down on or being seen as a failure not only excessively extol their own virtues, they often excessively point out the weaknesses of others.

Being self-deprecating occasionally will help us feel more relaxed and comfortable with ourselves. We'll realize that criticism of us, even self-criticism, doesn't result in some cataclysmic event. Thus, it lessens our fear of being seen as a failure, so we don't need always be trying to impress people. We'll realize that good people accept us for who we are, not for who we're intent on proving we are.

Summary

To have a full response repertoire, we should be able to:

1. Periodically want and request some "down time" from our significant other.

2. Openly talk of our failures to significant people in our inner circle.

5. Fear of Intimacy

Would you have trouble making this statement to your significant other? "I really enjoy being with you and I think about you a good deal. Actually, when I know I'm not going to see you for a while, sometimes I feel a little sad."

Who doesn't want to hear these words occasionally? Who doesn't hear these words occasionally? Those having significant others who fear intimacy. Those who fear intimacy deprive people in their inner circle of much of the meaning of life.

What does intimacy mean? Often, it means speaking of feelings, close, personal feelings, such as love and fear. How do we determine whether this potentially important person in our life fears intimacy? By talking occasionally about our feelings (especially our fears) and noting their reaction. Do they respond positively with their undivided attention, neutrally by changing the topic, or negatively by cracking a sarcastic joke? If it's either of the last two, they fear intimacy. We may even ask them what their greatest fear is. If they ridicule us, scoff, or change the topic, they fear intimacy.

What is a relationship like with a significant other who fears intimacy? Cold, factual, barren, and devoid of much of the richness of life. It's a life of "extinction," missing too much of those shared deeper feelings that are required for happiness in any relationship. Emotional responsiveness is not enough; people who fear intimacy can be quite expressive and emotionally responsive…but about a ball game, not a relationship.

Some Signs

The fear of intimacy once was a predominantly male preserve. It's now become gender-free. Be it the corporate climber, the aggressive lawyer, or the assembly line worker, many people are more comfortable in business situations, at sporting events with casual friends, at a movie, or even in a hospital during a crisis, than they are being alone with a significant other. In the last instance, the potential for intimacy is just too great.

The sarcastic, caustic person, the macho sportsman, and the "tough" cop, for example, often fear intimacy. Tender moments were avoided by their repressed and emotionally barren parents. Expressions of affection were embarrassing to their same-sex friends in high school, and were quickly and harshly ridiculed, often with cutting sarcasm.

The excessive behaviors (fanatic interest in sports) of some people are frequently driven by this avoidance of intimacy. Discussing ball scores or being sarcastic in a bantering manner with macho friends in a sports bar is comforting and less anxiety provoking than being responsible for intimate, personal moments. Is it hard to believe that some cops are less frightened of physical violence than of intimacy with someone of the opposite sex? Is it difficult to believe that some people fear being liked because expressions of "being liked" are too intimate and disquieting?

We must be certain that we're not a person who fears intimacy. How? By openly and spontaneously discussing our feelings with our significant other: our hopes, joys, fears, frustrations, and goals. By wanting to know—and asking about—the feelings of our significant other on these same topics. We need to respond, not with uneasiness, but with understanding, concern, respect, and interest when they tell us about their feelings.

Excessive Behavior

You: "Do you mind if I hold your hand?"

A fearful partner: "Why? Are your hands cold?" Or "Oh, not here; not now." Or "Why would you do that? I don't have any money in it."

Do you know critical, sarcastic people who fear intimacy? Ask them a question about anything other than themselves and they normally answer in a factual, straightforward, cooperative manner. They're usually respectful of your question and you. Do you want to elicit sarcasm from them? Ask them a question about themselves, their feelings, or about your relationship together. But first prepare for a sarcastic assault; you'll generally get it.

Do you know highly critical people? At what times are they critical? In personal areas? Do they make snide remarks during a movie about a love relationship? Reasonable people may be bored by the movie and quietly say so; fearful people are sarcastic or overly critical; they carry on too long…their behavior is uncalled for.

Is your lover patient, understanding, and filled with good advice about your problems at work? That makes them very appealing. But is your lover critical, abrupt and/or condescending about your personal problems with a roommate? About your parents' marital strife? About your best friend's problems with her fiance? They may fear intimacy.

Is your significant other sincerely interested in and enthusiastic about your raise, your promotion, and your completion of the triathalon? Is this person perfunctory, demeaning, or ridiculing about your fears of being alone, of the beauty of long-term personal relationships, of your concern over your father's health? They may fear intimacy, they may fear anything personal, and they may be passively aggressive in avoiding it.

Excessively Avoided Behavior

As we've seen, people who fear intimacy can be emotionally responsive, enthusiastic, caring, knowledgeable—basically everything we want in a person. They can be perfect in every area except intimacy.

(She, to him, while he, as usual, watches sports on TV):
"I love you."
"That's great. Come on, take that shot! Take the shot!"

"I've got a problem I'd like to talk to you about."
"Okay, but wait just a few minutes. There are only eight minutes left in the game."

People fearing intimacy avoid anything personal, anything "deep," anything "close." If they only could react with as much emotional responsiveness to the personal areas as they do to everything else, life with them would be wonderful indeed.

Being Liked

The fear of intimacy can be a result of the individual's fear of being disliked. Thus, people who fear intimacy can be quite understanding and sympathetic when we discuss our deep feelings about someone else, even an old flame. Our love of others brings an objective and/or sympathetic response that can't help drawing us closer to them. But as we get closer to experiencing and expressing a *liking for them*, they get more critical and more sarcastic.

Have you met people who are always critical, who always focus on the negative things about other people, whose sense of humor is usually sarcastic? Such people often have a quick mind, made more so by their frequent and interesting repartee with other negative people. Their excessive sarcasm elicits laughter but covers fear—a fear of being liked, a fear of intimacy. Their sarcasm and criticalness keep people at an emotional distance. The person who is frequently sarcastic is often trying to prevent "mushy" conversations and interactions.

6. Fear of Being Disliked

Would you have a problem making this remark to someone important in your life: "I have to tell you what I feel is one of your shortcomings, and frankly, it's been bothering me for a while now."

Do you have difficulty saying this? You may have a fear of being disliked.

Living in a vacuum with no input from others about who you are (in their eyes) leads to rapid deterioration and isolation from reality. Any solid relationship requires that we be able to give our significant other negative feedback occasionally. If we don't, who will? But we won't be able to give them meaningful and constructive feedback if we fear being disliked by them. Consequently, they'll become more and more unaware of who they are and what impact they have on other people. A fear of being disliked does no one any favors, especially those in one's inner circle.

Some Causes

In contrast to the person who fears intimacy, those who fear being disliked were often raised in punitive, sometimes emotionally volatile homes. The children were punished often, sometimes physically, but more often by parental withdrawal and/or pouting. The parents were easily frustrated and readily expressed their frustrations, even though it might have been in subtle ways.

The peers of these children quickly learned of the children's fear of being disliked and used that knowledge to dominate them. The person who fears being disliked often becomes a "pawn," subject to the whims and desires of others.

Some Consequences

Many of us seek out as friends people who fear being disliked. They're often placating, easy to control, ready to subscribe to our wishes and desires. They do not have the "normal" desire to be liked. Hence, people who fear being disliked avoid at all cost doing anything that might displease others. Thus, they are easily seduced, both mentally and physically. So we feel quite comfortable with them. But this is a mistake for everyone.

Can we imagine living a life with someone who agreed with everything we did, with every belief we held, with every action we took? It's the very thing dreams are made of, right? Not really. We'd be bored stiff and would soon listen to our partner with as much enthusiasm as we'd listen to a lecture on nailing tapioca to the wall. We'd know their opinion before they expressed it. Their views would be boring, meaningless, and we wouldn't take them seriously.

People who fear being disliked offer little to others. One of the great assets of a significant other is that they have our best interests at heart. This means they give us realistically constructive feedback, even in negative areas. A key result of this behavior is that we'll grow at a personal level. By keeping us in touch with reality, they help us to be more effective. People who fear being disliked by us do few of these things. They may lead us to feel superior when we're with them, but other people are unlikely to see us as such.

Excessive Behaviors

All of us want to influence people, each of us for different reasons (mostly to prevent others from engaging in the behavior we fear). Who gives us more control over them than someone who fears being disliked by us?

But what if someone continually inquires about our desires, needs, and concerns? Is that really behaving inappropriately? This could be difficult to accept. However, the boredom of the relationship would lead us to become frustrated and angry. Many of us want a rich life that stimulates us to grow and develop. The person who fears being disliked is excessively bland and cannot offer us that.

Two managers in an extremely successful company held a "town meeting," each with his own subordinates. The company was "jumping," had made several major discoveries, was getting unusually favorable press, and was being looked on as the premier organization in its field. One manager told his group how wonderful everyone in the company was and that even greater successes lay ahead of them. It was quite inspirational and motivational, and he was loved by all.

The second manager told his group that they should realize that they were not that important to anyone outside the company. He emphasized the point that if they were to disappear from the earth tomorrow, most people's lives would go on as before. He was neither as inspirational nor as loved.

Who is the better manager? The second. He recognized that extreme success often breeds arrogance in organizations (and individuals), an arrogance that frequently leads employees to start treating customers with disdain and lack of consideration. The second manager tried to give his people a sense of reality so that their premier position would not lead to catastrophic failure, as it so often does with companies that (or people who) experience unparalleled success. The first manager, because of his fear of being disliked, led the employees down an unrealistic path, one that could lead to serious problems.

Suppose those around us, those whom we've picked for our inner circle, fear being disliked by us. They will placate us, regardless of what we do or say. Then we'll run the danger of becoming arrogant and unrealistic in our expectations of others. And we'll risk losing good friends. A relationship should be a partnership, a give-and-take of reasonable proportions and mutually constructive feedback. One-sided relationships (those built with people who fear us disliking them) lack balance, symmetry, and a mutual sense of challenge and growth.

Persons who always have their way because they've picked fearful people for their inner circle will become spoiled children. They will soon expect everyone to treat them with the same deference and awe as their fearful friends do. The college football hero who enters the cold reality of the business world sometimes learns this lesson the hard way. The excessive admiration and accolades are suddenly gone, too often resulting in frustration and depression, sure precursors of failure.

Excessively Avoided Behavior

People who fear being disliked generally won't criticize others; it's not in their repertoire. When they gave honest feedback, too often they encountered dislike or even hostility. We will get only *good* (gentle but constructive) criticism from people who truly care about us and sincerely want to help us. And realistic feedback is the best source of personal growth for anyone; realistic feedback is to the soul what food is to the body.

If we dislike the person who offers us constructive criticism, we are being driven by our fear. Individuals who lack a fear of being disliked by us are often invaluable. They are frequently the source of open, honest feedback, without which we would function in a "vacuum." And vacuums lead to a lack of awareness of reality and our place in it. (If a person is excessively critical of us, then their behavior is being driven by a destructive fear, such as the fear of intimacy discussed above.)

Summary

Having a wide response repertoire should allow us to:

1. Express our deepest feelings to our significant others with neither inhibition nor embarrassment.

2. Gently, but openly, give those close to us constructive feedback that enables them to adapt more effectively to reality.

Chapter Six

7. Fear of Making a Commitment

Are you able to make this proposal to your significant other?

"You're very important to me. If you'd feel comfortable if we dated only each other, let's do it."

This comment comes from a person who does not fear what many do—**making a commitment**. Many of us fear a *lack* of commitment by others. But many of us fear *making* a commitment to others, especially significant others. Indeed, few things between men and women elicit more violent clashes than this fear. That's because both sides of this fear often involve numerous other fears.

Some Causes

Parents who frequently argue, pout, separate, and/or divorce create an atmosphere in which commitment becomes "scary." Even long-term friendships that are split apart, especially by uncontrollable factors (such as one person moving away), can lead to a subconscious hesitation over potential relationships.

Because our fears basically revolve around the behavior of other people, many of the fears we experience will influence our orientation toward commitment. Those who fear making a commitment often fear such things as intimacy, being controlled, boredom, being insignificant to others ("how many will **not** love me if I'm already taken?"), being responsible for those who want a commitment from them (emotionally and economically), or being seen as a failure (many marriages end in divorce). Those who fear a lack of commitment by their significant others often fear being alone, economic deprivation, being rejected or disliked, lack of control, or being insignificant to someone special.

Is it any wonder that the concept of marriage (THE commitment) often proves to be the ultimate battleground? Thus, it's important to determine a person's fears (our own included). We'll be in a better position to determine how those fears will affect people's reaction to commitment and how their fears will influence the need for—and ability to make—a commitment.

Some Consequences

A realistic evaluation of ourselves and our significant other is crucial in this area if we want to avoid the trap of wasting years of our lives and the lives of those around us on unattainable goals. If a person fears making a commitment, that fear—and the fears driving it—will probably have been apparent throughout the individual's life. Unstable work histories, high-risk business ventures, failure to meet or even enter into long-term obligations (car or house payments), failure to fulfill obligations (dates or appointments), many short-lived relationships—all indicate fear of commitment.

Yet, people who won't make a commitment are often attractive lovers. They can be very exciting. Their high-risk orientation and lack of need to control others makes them quite flexible and tolerant in relationships. They're sometimes so pleasant and tolerant that it's difficult to see that their graciousness comes from their lack of emotional involvement. They are interested in many areas of life (but none too deeply), a fact that also makes them interesting. They are easy-going people, adept at meeting others because they meet new people so often. They're good people to everyone at a superficial level and to no one at a deeper level...a level that might involve commitment.

Excessive Behaviors

Does your significant other like John Wayne movies (or similar others)? Why? Because John usually rides off into the sunset with his trusted horse, beholden only to the sunset and the beast he's sitting on.

What are John Wayne characters noted for? Independence. Being their own man. Needing no one. If our "significant other" frequently extols the virtues of the noble cowboy and/or his philosophy, it may be because of his **fear of commitment**.

Does our significant other like tennis, boxing, anything that is not a "team" sport? Is he an entrepreneur and insistent that he remain so, despite attractive offers from organizations? Is he afraid of depending on others, afraid of having to rely on his colleagues to do their job in order to get his done? Is he fearful of being placed in a position of needing others in order to get what he wants? Does he often speak of how undependable people are?

Does he talk of how others need him, never of how he needs others? Does he generally pair or associate "having to depend on others" with negatives? "The guy promised on his mother's grave that he'd have that report done. Because he didn't, I lost the job. People are so damned unreliable." Does he frequently and too aggressively associate such things as marriage or a business partnership with negatives? Does he too often admire the iconoclast, the rebel? He may be fearful of commitment, of needing someone.

Excessively Avoided Behavior

Can our significant other say, "I need your help"? Can he tell anyone he needs them? The excessive avoidance of any sign of needing others is a strong sign of the fear of commitment.

Can he say, "Joe is really better at this than I am."? Can he accept the fact that some people could do a better job than he could in some areas? Can he ever extol the virtues of others in comparison with himself? If he cannot, he may well fear making a commitment, since others are so "incapable of giving him anything."

This person's employer wants him to sign a two-year employment agreement, but he backed off, saying, "No way could I trust the company." He wanted the car, but getting it would have involved a long-term financial commitment in the form of monthly payments. He didn't buy it. He owes no one anything and never will. He loved the woman, but being with her would have meant helping raise her six-year old. Too big a commitment. Any commitment is nothing but trouble to him. Even a long-term relationship is just not in his response repertoire.

The fear of making a commitment is becoming more prevalent in society for a number of reasons. Today's intensely competitive economic environment is raising monetary fears in everyone. Those who seek out marriage frequently do so to increase their economic security. Those who avoid marriage frequently do so because of the responsibility (including economic) they would assume.

But much more important is the underlying and pervasive fear of being controlled. Many people disrespect and fear anyone's trying to exert control over them, from politicians to bosses, from parents to siblings, from spouses to children. Being told they must make a commitment is the same as telling them someone wants to control them. And often someone does. Actually, everyone with whom we interact would like to control us in some way. The only reason we make these sounds we call "words" is to influence someone. The more dainty among us may want to call it education or persuasiveness or inspirational speech-making. But the real goal is to influence, to control. And everyone wants to, tries to, and often succeeds, despite protests to the contrary. We may have different goals and say different things in going about trying to influence people, but we all want to influence them. Actions do not speak louder than words; words are action, and their impact on people can be just as great.

Those who focus on others and evaluate them accurately will usually respond effectively and appropriately to the fears of the other person, instead of being driven to ineffective behaviors by their own fears. Those who are driven only by their own fears will engage in excessive, fear-driven behaviors. Those who seek to influence someone who fears making a commitment, for example, are too often responding to their own fear of lacking control or feeling insignificant. Responding to their own fear leads them into excessive behaviors, which are, of course, promptly interpreted as overly controlling by the recipient (which they are, because they are based on fear). This too often ensures conflict and a lack of commitment.

8. Fear of Being Alone

Would you be able to make this suggestion to your most significant other? "I'd really like to be alone for a bit. Could we hold off getting together for a few days?"

Is this tough to say? If so, you may have one of the most pervasive of all fears, the **fear of being alone.**

Some Causes

Why do we have this fear? Do we dislike the company we're with when we're alone? When we were little did the dark scare us when we were alone? Did we feel that everyone was bigger than us and there was no possible way we could protect ourself from all the evils of life? We were right. No wonder we feared being alone!

But then isn't now. Many fears are learned in childhood. And often these fears are quite appropriate and realistic for an early age. Fear's tenacity, however, is startling. And the fear of being alone is one of the most tenacious and pervasive of all fears.

Some Consequences

Why is the fear of being alone so important? Because it drives so many other fears. Our fear of confrontation, of being rejected or of being considered insignificant, for example, often develop because these situations have led to our being alone. Mary refused to play with us; Jean didn't return our calls; Michelle wouldn't talk to us. The result was...we would end up alone and feeling unworthy. Soon we did anything to avoid Mary's rejection, Jean's indifference, Michelle's anger.

Suppose you knew with absolutely no doubt that you would spend the rest of your life without any significant other, no one to love you and share life with you. Suppose that your life would be perfectly normal, except that you would never be that special someone to anyone. Is that a devastating thought?

Would you find as much pleasure in romantic novels, movies, and TV plays with emotional love scenes (which is most of them)? Would you feel somewhat helpless and highly vulnerable? Would your interests in life change dramatically? Would your daydreams change? Would you be depressed? Frustrated?

Actually, these scenarios are not that far from reality. Many people end up "alone," even those who are married. Yet most of us have hope. We all have our dreams, our desires, our lusts, our need to impress, be significant and important. The behaviors we engage in daily because of our need to avoid being alone are startling.

Freedom from the Fear of Being Alone

But what would happen if we did not fear being alone? What would happen if we did not expect to ever have or even meet "Mr(s). Wonderful," someone to whom we are very important? What would happen if we truly believed that no one would ever be that important to us nor us to them? Certainly our expectations would drop. In fact, our expectations might become more realistic. Maybe we would become less frustrated and less fearful, more calmly contented, and confident.

That's how people who do not have the fear of being alone, rare as they may be, frequently feel. They often have a wide-ranging set of interests. Many things in the world fascinate them, people most of all. But instead of caring so much what people think of them, they just enjoy people for who they are. There is no need to impress, minimal need to criticize, little that is disliked, and much that is sincerely respected. There is no need to control, no fear of being controlled or being insignificant or being disliked, minimal striving. In sum, they are much happier. And if your *fear* of being alone is diminished, even a little bit, your joy will be commensurately increased. Why? Because so many of our common fears are based on the fear of being alone.

If we want to try to reach this goal, we'll need help. But if we try to enlist the help of our best friends, we'll probably be punished greatly. Why? Because our friends probably share our fear of not having someone "who's their own" in their life. We probably share many experiences with them over the significant others (or potential ones) in our lives. If we tell them that we want to rid ourselves of that fear and don't want to go on striving to find "the right one," we'll probably break one of the great common bonds between us and them, the fear of being alone. So they'll punish us for having so horrendous a thought; it scares them, since we might be saying that we won't find them significant anymore.

Excessive Behaviors

Is someone placating, needful of attention, intent on impressing, preoccupied with their physical looks, punishing of anyone who likes others or even themselves, sensitive to rejection or criticism, too concerned with disappointing others? Then they fear being alone. Actually, this fear is so prevalent and basic that almost any excessive (fear-driven) behavior can probably be partially blamed on it.

But those who fear being alone often trip themselves up in the "love relationship" area. Why? Because their fear of being alone often leads them to be excessive, e.g., smothering, in their attempts to be with someone. Thus, people avoid them. The person who fears being alone too frequently imposes on others' time.

Another behavior resulting from this fear is the building of an infra-structure of groups and activities that almost precludes the person from dating, even though the person wants to date someone "more than any-thing." Their fear of being alone, however, has led to many superficial commitments (more than almost anyone can handle). This almost ensures their being alone in terms of a significant other.

"Would you like to go to a show Tuesday?"

"I'm sorry, I'm going out with the other teachers for dinner that night."

"How about Wednesday?"

"Gee, I told my sister I would take my niece out that night."

"Well, how about Thursday?"

"Oh, that's the night my ski club meets."

"That leaves Friday."

"I'm sorry. It's usually not like this, really, but my book club meets that Friday."

"Well, maybe I'll call you again sometime."

The person who is frequently unavailable to the invitations of potential significant others is the person we stop inviting out (if we're confident). Their fear of being alone gets them what they fear.

Excessively Avoided Behavior

Have you ever gone *alone* to a movie or play or dinner? Were you comfortable doing it? Someone who fears being alone doesn't feel com-fortable and rarely does it. Is being alone and reading a good novel or listening to some favorite music late at night a treat? Not to someone who fears being alone. These are great pastimes and they should be part of everyone's repertoire.

Tired of this fear? Consider whatever you would like to do with a significant other and try it alone. Want to walk along the beach with someone? Try it alone. Want to see a good movie with that special person? Try it alone. Want to have a leisurely meal with someone at a favorite restaurant? Try it alone. You might actually enjoy it.

Who are You with When You're Alone?

We also fear being alone because we don't like the people we're with when we are alone...ourselves (this point is so important that it will be covered more extensively in chapter 14). Why are we so inclined to dislike ourselves? Because too many people in our inner circle, those who have such a strong influence on us, don't want us to like ourselves. They fear being insignificant to us, being disliked by us, lacking influence over us, and they fear our rejection and our criticism. If we don't like ourselves, our friends often feel (subconsciously) that we will need them.

This often occurs with spouses and parents of adult children. If spouses and/or parents frequently criticize us, they subconsciously think our lack of confidence will lead us to need them. Not liking or trusting ourselves, we'll be more comfortable only if they're near by. And so we'll constantly seek them out, asking for their guidance, opinions, their concerns and desires.

How do they criticize us? By associating us and/or our actions with negatives:

> "You really don't do too well at that sort of thing."
>
> "You can be so childish at times."
>
> "Why didn't you call me? Sometimes, you're really a very inconsiderate, thoughtless person."
>
> "You certainly have a lot to learn."
>
> "Well, the last time you picked the restaurant, and you remember what a disaster that was!"

"Can't you do anything right!?"

"Why would you say such a stupid thing?"

"I'm really surprised at how you dress—you really don't have much of an aesthetic sense, do you?"

"I would really appreciate it if you didn't say anything to him; you really embarrass me at times."

Watch out for the especially pernicious "but" associations:

"Well, people may seem to like you, *but* that's because they don't see who you really are and how superficial you can be."

"You did get a nice car, *but* you spent way too much for it; you got taken. You should have really asked me before you got it."

"That's a nice blouse, *but* you really didn't match it very well with your slacks."

"You may be more emotionally responsive than me, *but* you're a lot more critical of people than I am."

Our difficulty in being comfortable with ourselves is tied directly to the feeling of people around us that their fears will be lessened if we dislike ourselves and need them. Do your parents fear being insignificant to you? They'll associate "you" ("you never call") with negatives (the definition of guilt). Does your significant other fear being insignificant to you? Being rejected by you? Being criticized by you? Being seen as a failure by you? They'll associate "you" with negatives. This will be disastrous for you. And because their you-negative associations are being driven by fear, they will be excessively frequent. And so the fears of those in our inner circle are visited upon us!

(To experience a true shock, focus on your closest friend periodically and note the number of you-negative associations made toward you. No wonder so many of us dislike ourselves, lack confidence, and fear being alone.)

Learning To Like Ourselves

Whenever someone says "you," we need to listen closely. If they associate "you" with a positive, we should seek them out, appreciate them, express our feelings openly to them, and interact frequently with them. Then we'll learn to like and be comfortable with the one person from whom we can never escape, the one person who is always with us.

Interacting with people who have the confidence to compliment others, and making them feel comfortable doing so with us by emotionally reinforcing them, should be an integral part of our response inventory, readily and easily called forth when appropriate.

(This is one reason it's important to lessen our inhibitions over responding emotionally. Emotional responses are generally reinforcing to people and enable us to strengthen the behavior in others that will help us. Our emotional response to compliments, for example, increases the frequency of this behavior in others. This will go a long way toward increasing our confidence and decreasing our fears, especially our fear of being alone.)

If "you" is too often associated by certain individuals with negatives, we should run from them. Their fear will make us fearful and distrustful of the one most important thing we have in life, the one thing from which we can never escape...ourself.

Can we get our pride and our confidence back? Yes, if we seek out as friends people who reinforce our love of ourselves and our love of other good people in our lives.

It may well be that the fear of being alone has led more people to do more self-destructive things (in order to placate or please others) than any other fear. To avoid being alone, for example, we may content ourselves with destructive people as our friends. Being destructive and wanting us dependent on them, they criticize us too much. Thus, we learn to dislike ourselves more and continue to add more destructive people to our inner circle. And so the cycle spins on.

Summary

Over the next few weeks, we should be able to tell our significant other:

1. That we made some type of long-term commitment (e.g., borrowed some money from them and made a long-term payment plan to pay it back...with interest).

2. That we need some time for ourselves, time to be alone for a little while.

If we hesitate with either of these, we're probably touching one of our fears.

Chapter Seven

9. Fear of Disappointing Others

Can you say this to your significant other? "I know it's a special day for you, but I really feel that I must finish this work. If I celebrate with you now, I'll never get it done."

Can we disappoint someone we like, someone who is close to us? Do we have trouble standing up for what we want, knowing the other person will look downcast and downtrodden—all because of our "selfishness"? For many, the **fear of disappointing significant others** is a powerful one.

Those who are fearful of disappointing important people in their lives give up a good deal of control to them. Spouses and bosses are especially relevant. They fill the two major roles of intimacy and authority that the parents filled initially. As a result, the fear of disappointing others learned in childhood is often most pronounced with spouses and bosses later in life.

Some Causes

Raised in homes where emotional expressiveness rarely occurred, the children had few clues indicating how others (especially parents) were feeling about them. As a result, the children often became highly sensitive to subtle indexes of approval or disapproval. Minute signs of disappointment had as much impact on them as the screaming of a more overtly abusive parent.

This is particularly true in the case of a father and daughter. Men have been taught not to be emotionally responsive and they have also learned to fear intimacy generally, especially with women. The uncomfortable feelings of love felt for his daughter often influence a father's emotional withdrawal from her. The father's philosophy: Best to "clam up." Best not to say anything. Best to let "the wife" handle the kids' upbringing.

And where does that leave the daughter? In a vacuum. In a life where the only anchors, the only signposts with men, are the subtle nuances they give off. It was that "little grimace" over the "B" in the midst of all those "A's," that "subtle turning away" when she came home late, that "small sigh" when she wanted to quit her part-time job at the fast food restaurant. And since her father's only "reaction" consisted of these subtle gestures of disappointment over her behavior, that's the thing to which she developed an exquisite sensitivity. Her sensitivity is now focused on what men in general and her significant other in particular think of her and her behavior.

Women are more susceptible to this fear precisely because men are taught to avoid feelings. As a result, few men are even aware of disappointment in others, let alone being influenced adversely by it.

Some Consequences

People who fear disappointing significant others are frequently liked and sought out by others. This is because their fear of disappointing people often leads to a pleasing subservience and exquisite thoughtfulness. This intensely cooperative spirit makes them wonderful partners and superb employees. They are generally quite "sweet" and follow rules and regulations closely. They rarely complain.

There are three negative consequences to having them as a significant other or an employee:

1. People with the fear of disappointing significant others can be boring over the long haul. People who know them only superficially and don't interact with them frequently adore them. But those with a fear of disappointing readily become dependent on the suggestions, ideas, desires, and whims of others, especially significant others and bosses. People with the fear of disappointing others have little independence, minimal initiative, and little to contribute to a relationship or an organization.

2. People who fear disappointing others give minimal constructive input to others. Although they can readily admire and appreciate others, they rarely criticize or confront. As a result, those with this fear make little contribution to the growth of anyone or anything. As providers of the constructive feedback that we all need, they are of little value. Their views on life and most things in it merely mirror the views of those they don't want to disappoint.

3. People who fear disappointing others are often, like their parents, emotionally non-responsive. Because an emotional reaction is *the* positive reinforcer to most people, dealing with them frequently leads to the frustration felt at **not** being reinforced. In other words, people with this fear "extinguish" the behavior of people with their constant non-responsiveness, and this "extinction" always leads to frustration.

This frustration will then lead to the anger typical of those who must deal daily with emotionally non-responsive extinguishers. Soon we'll see the hostile, abusive mate who is always criticizing this quiet, loving, thoughtful person. Who among us doesn't know an abusive husband, always criticizing his spouse, one of the sweetest women we ever met? And why is he abusive? In great part, because the sweet wife is so quiet, and so emotionally non-responsive.

In some situations, we often wonder how such a loving, kind and considerate woman can continue to live with such a "jerk," especially when we know the jerk is a philandering, undependable, overly negative, inconsiderate slob. It's because those traits in him don't bother her. What bothers her is anything *she* does that might elicit disappointment from him.

Excessive Behavior

Excessive behavior in a person with the fear of disappointing others take the form of whatever behavior accomplishes that goal with the significant other. The fact that she forgot to bring his coat, that she didn't have dinner on time—whatever he feels disappointment over because of **her behavior**—is what she will focus on.

Was he disappointed because she was late? She will now be compulsively on time. He soon learns that his silence and subtle disapproval (a sort of pouting) will immediately give him a good deal of control over her. Was he overly quiet and non-responsive because she didn't have dinner on time? She bought a hotplate and obsesses about timely dinners now. "What did I do wrong?" she constantly asks.

In addition, this fear frequently generalizes to a sensitivity to the disappointment of other people, especially in areas that may not be significant to others. How did the teacher feel about the paper I wrote? How did the waiter feel about the tip I left?

Excessively Avoided Behavior

A person with the fear of disappointing doesn't complain about anything their significant other does, no matter how egregious. He/she may come home late for dinner or bring home unannounced guests without calling. No problem. As long as he/she doesn't show disappointment.

But suppose he grows unnaturally quiet about the meal? That dinner will never be made again. Suppose he doesn't criticize an outfit but merely looks away quietly when asked for an opinion about it. The outfit probably won't be worn again—at least in his presence. Silence and apparent disappointment is too much to handle. In sum, the person who fears the disappointment of their partner is preoccupied with their *own* behavior and obsessively avoids engaging in any behavior that elicits the dreaded disappointment from the partner—which can be almost anything!

The fear of disappointing others reflects the epitome of guilt. It's *my* behavior that causes others' pain. It's *my* behavior that's evil and wrong. Because people with this fear are taught that there are so many things they do that are "bad," people who fear disappointing others are left with a very narrow response repertoire. Hence their "quietness."

10. Fear of Being Seen as Weak or Frightened

Can you say to your significant other, "You know what? Those guys seem to be looking for a fight. I'm getting nervous. Let's get out of here."

For the true-blue American male, this is probably a difficult thing to say. How many men have the confidence to say they're afraid, especially to a significant other? None who are macho. None who fear that someone, especially a significant other, will **see them as weak or frightened**.

The fear of being seen as weak or frightened is so prevalent among males that few can escape it. This fear is often the motivator for "heroism" on the battlefield. Many men would rather risk death than the possibility that their peers would see them as fearful.

Some Causes

This fear almost seems genetic because it's so dysfunctional, yet it is ingrained and pervasive in our male population. Few boys escape childhood without being accused periodically by peers of the worst possible sin—being a "sissy," chicken (yellow, spineless, wimp, and 600 other descriptive terms making the same point). With such a premium placed on *not* being weak or frightened, it's a wonder any young men survive into adulthood.

Many of the dangers faced in childhood and adolescence are real. We can be ordered about in punishing ways, even slapped or spanked, beaten up, shot at, and all experience many other sorts of calamities without having many resources to protect us. Who will protect us from an abusive parent? From an unfair, hypercritical teacher? How can anyone protect us from a "drive by" shooting? Teenagers can be a violent lot indeed, especially toward those who frighten them most—usually other teenagers.

Some Consequences

The ridicule boys experience from their peers (and fathers) for being afraid is ever-present. The resulting fear of the possibility of being seen as frightened readily carries over into most men's interactions with females. And, because women rarely experience the fear of being seen as frightened, it's often little understood by females, just as the fear of disappointing others is little understood by many men.

Women may not care whether their man is "tough," but readily feel the consequences as their significant others strut about, swaggering with the surge of testosterone. Certainly a great deal of pain, suffering, even death, came as a result of someone's trying to prove he was not "chicken," that he was not afraid. Proving what to whom? Does he want to be seen as brave? No. He's just afraid of being seen as weak or frightened. And that's why his behavior becomes exaggerated and dangerous.

Many women don't appreciate how widespread and intense this fear is in men. Most women could elicit a lot of love from many men by remarking occasionally on how strong and masculine, or how tough and bold, their partner is. "You're one of the most confident men I've ever met," is almost always certain to elicit intense devotion from most males. Why? Because the woman is temporarily alleviating a potent fear, one that is almost universal in the male population, the fear of appearing weak.

The Battle of the Sexes

Most friendships are based on the common bond of similar fears. We often feel patience and tolerance, even camaraderie, toward those who share our fears. Patience and tolerance, however, are rarely felt toward the fears of others that we don't share. Frustration over their "silly" behavior is more likely.

In the formative years, boys are often influenced by boys and girls by girls. This results in the camaraderie seen in same-sex friendships, an intimacy that those of the opposite sex aren't expected to share or even understand. Because the sexes often do not share the same fears, the result is often frustration, anger, ridicule, and overly critical attitudes between significant others (hence "Men are from Mars...").

Often, a man's behavior toward a woman is determined by his concern with what other *men* will think of him because he has her on his arm. Indeed, the woman a man wants for a wife often has more to do with what he feels his other male friends will think of him because of her presence and looks than with who she truly is and will be to him.

Because women's fears, conversely, were often initiated and strengthened in early years by girlfriends, their particular fears are little understood and less tolerated by men. Are women in the room noticing who I'm with? Are they disappointed by him? Will others criticize or ridicule me tomorrow for being desperate because I'm with him?

Excessive Behavior

Those who excessively try to prevent being seen as frightened are our so-called macho friends:

"Did you see that blitz in the third quarter? I thought our middle linebacker was going to take his head off! Man, it was a great game."

"Did you see him highstick the guy in the third period? I thought he was going to shove the puck down the jerk's throat."

To whom are these things said on a frequent, repetitive basis? The friends of the macho male, his inner circle. Who are his friends? Other macho males, those who share his fears of being seen as frightened. That's why they're his friends. And in whose presence does he also show this macho behavior? When he's with his significant other.

Why are violent sports such strong reinforcers to our macho friends? Because violent sports alleviate the macho person's fear of **being seen** as frightened and weak. Only "tough" people in the sports bar take delight in such violence as a hockey game or football. Because friendship is often based on shared interests—and shared interests are often based on shared fears—everyone reinforces everyone else in the sports bar for their fears and already exaggerated behavior.

Excessively Avoided Behavior

Macho men obviously avoid admitting being fearful or frightened. But intimacy, affection, and the sharing of feelings are also associated with "wimps." Thus, people with the fear of being seen as weak can never know the joy of these deeper, more meaningful experiences. "Real men" watching a football game don't often speak to each other at half-time about their affections and fears (unless it's in a derogatory, ridiculing manner.

Men with the fear of being seen as frightened are confined to the narrow world of the strong and the brave, the tough and the independent, but all to excess and all to the exclusion of other satisfactions.

"Damn, I was really frightened then."

"Well, I saw the guy was probably a weight-lifter and could wipe up the floor with my little body in about 30 seconds. So I graciously said he could have any chair he wanted, including mine."

"The word 'fear' is not in my vocabulary...now the word 'terror' is, and I use that a lot."

"Actually, I always get nervous when I'm going to give a speech."

These people must be frightened; after all, they just said so. Not really. *Behaviorally*, (see chapter 17) these people are confident. After all, they have the confidence to tell someone they are frightened at times (is there someone who isn't?). Those who cannot confess to their fears occasionally have a narrowed response repertoire, a sure sign of fear.

Summary

Can we engage in behaviors that disappoint significant others by occasionally not meeting their expectations or their requests of us?

Chapter Eight

11. Fear of Confrontation

Can you say this to someone important (a boss?) in your life? "You've been accusing me lately of some things that I feel are untrue. I'd like to talk about those accusations now."

Who likes to be disliked? Actually, some people do. Everything is reinforcing to someone (even pain or death), and nothing is reinforcing to everyone. Not many of us, however, want to face someone who is angry with us. We certainly learned earlier, with parents, teachers, and other authority figures, that their anger often left us on the losing side. We have developed, as a result, a **fear of confrontation.**

Some Causes

Fear of someone's anger is quite common, especially in people who have been raised by abusive parents. Although this is similar to the fear of being disliked, the fear of confrontation involves more the fear of the sudden emotional component, the unexpected anger of someone close or important.

Anger and ridicule (punishment) from other people are often unusually influential in shaping early attitudes. Many of us quickly learn which behaviors to avoid in order to prevent anger and ridicule. Boys, for example, often ridicule other boys for being enthusiastic or positive about anything. Being critical is a sign of "toughness." Most women, on the other hand, are punished by parents and teachers for using negatives; they seem to be held to a higher standard in this area

than boys. Hence, women frequently have difficulty expressing negatives. The fear of confrontation, consequently, is found more frequently
in women.

Some Consequences

Fear of confrontation can be a dangerous fear, one that will make us
likely to become nervous and upset when another person is angry and
hostile toward us. Thus, we reinforce and thereby *strengthen* the other
person's hostility toward us. If we fear confrontation, the anger of hostile people in our inner circle will probably become more frequent.

If someone frequently and repetitively reacts with criticism or
ridicule (anger) when we're enthusiastic, we might be headed for a life
with them that could be most destructive. If we also fear confronting
the angry person over their behavior (often the appropriate response),
a positive relationship is virtually impossible. Women who remain
with physically abusive husbands sometimes do so to avoid the antici-
pated confrontation that they fear would happen if they left (or took
any constructive action). Their fear of confrontation keeps them in the
relationship—for more physical abuse.

If a woman fears confrontation, she hands over a great deal of control to others. Her reluctance to use negatives, which *must* be used by
everyone periodically, too often precludes others from taking her
seriously. It lessens her significance and impact on others. Thus,
many women's fear of confrontation almost ensures that they won't
take an authoritative approach when appropriate. This thickens the
glass ceiling. It should be noted that confronting someone even once
will have a long-term impact. It tells others that confrontations are
always possible with this person.

The fear of confrontation in the business setting, for example,
accounts for many disasters. It prevents people from speaking up to their
boss (authority figure), thus depriving that boss of needed feedback.

Knowing that they should have spoken up but didn't further drains the confidence of the employee. Although we pick as friends those who share our fears, we often pick as lovers those whom we hope will lessen our fears. (This expectation is rarely satisfied, hence the difficulties of personal relationships.) Consequently, people who fear confrontation often pick abusive people as a significant other. Their fear of confrontation leads them to select someone who is supposedly confident, i.e., someone who doesn't fear confrontation. The abusive person obviously doesn't show fear of confrontation. After all, they're frequently hostile and abusive with people and couldn't possibly fear confrontations.

The abusive person's behavior is geared to elicit confrontations (but only with "weak" people, a fact the fearful person rarely comprehends, since they fear it with everyone). This "strong (abusive) person" will then protect the fearful person, they hope, from confrontations with others. Thus does a fear of confrontation sometimes lead us to seek out what we think is confidence, but what is really fear-driven, abusive, and exaggerated confrontational behavior.

Excessive Behaviors

What might a person who fears confrontation do excessively that prevents confrontations? Placating, excessively diffident and sub-servient behavior come immediately to mind. Alcoholic husbands (who are often passive-aggressive), the alcohol diminishing their fears and inhibitions over expressing their anger, often use the wife's fear of confrontation to maintain a dominance over her. The wife's cowed reaction reinforces and strengthens the husband's drunken anger.

Humor As Defense

Could you get angry with, confront, or ridicule someone who always made you laugh, and at their expense, not yours? Many people "defang" an enemy by initiating frequent, repetitive humor, humor that is often directed at themselves in a self-deprecating way. Overweight people sometimes do this.

A consultant was once asked to counsel a corporate lawyer who would not speak up at meetings. Not speaking up could be fatal to an attorney who, like all lawyers, is expected to say "no" quite often. The consultant expected to find a shy, withdrawn person hiding in the corner. Quite the contrary, the attorney was warm, friendly, and outgoing. Not only was she outgoing, it turned out that she was a professional comedienne who, in the evening, would stand on stage alone and ad-lib on topics spontaneously thrown out by her audience. Questioned about her inhibitions in business meetings, she responded quizzically, "I really don't know why I can't speak up here."

The answer finally appeared: This woman feared confrontations. That's why she was a comedienne (making people laugh precludes confrontations). As a lawyer, speaking up would often necessitate adversarial interactions, i.e., confrontations. Many people who use humor excessively, especially self-deprecating (but not sarcastic) humor, do so to prevent confrontation.

Excessively Avoided Behavior

The behavior avoided in order to sidestep confrontations is often rampant in both our lives and the lives of our friends. People who fear confrontations rarely argue a point, criticize a fault in others, or make requests of others to help them achieve their own goals—reasonable as these requests might be. Those who fear confrontations are a "cork in the sea," being tossed to and fro by the desires of those with whom they fear confrontation. They are always on guard, sensitive to any sign of impending anger by someone, anyone. They rarely ask for a raise or promotion, even when it's more than justified. They wouldn't dream of criticizing anyone. Asking them what "our greatest shortcoming is" in order to get needed feedback is a futile request.

Fear of confrontation often leads others to more readily confront the fearful person rather than more confident individuals, especially when they want something unreasonable. Because fear-driven persons too often back away from fighting for what is rightfully theirs, they're more easily taken advantage of by those who know of their fear. In a competitive society such as ours, this can prove to be disastrous.

Confrontations are especially difficult when they involve authority figures. Fearing the wrath and criticism of his superior over possible mistakes from his department often encourages a manager to be perfectionistic with subordinates. However, these managers are more likely to be hypercritical, overly demanding, and petty with subordinates who are placating and subservient with their superiors. So the petty and perfectionist manager is driven to be so by both the demands of his superior and the fear of confrontation of his subordinate. (Sometimes, it's better to just leave the position in order to protect our confidence.)

Confrontations are an unpleasant but necessary part of life, especially with those closest and most important to us. If we are to have a wide response repertoire, the ability to confront must be an integral part of it.

12. Fear of Meeting New People

Can you say this to another person? "I'd love to go to the party. There will be a lot of people there I don't know, so it should be a real kick."

Life is little more than a series of interpersonal exchanges. These interactions have a great influence on us, who we are, how we feel about ourselves and others, and about life generally. It would seem beneficial, therefore, to have as many diverse people in our lives as possible. This would give us a support network of alternatives, of different people to help strengthen us and broaden our responses in different areas. Yet some studies have shown that the two greatest and most prevalent fears are: being alone and—**fear of meeting new people!**

Signs of the Fear of Meeting New People

This fear is betrayed in the following types of comments:

"Oh, I really don't want to go on a blind date. They can be so disastrous."

"I'd like to meet your friends some time, but not just yet. It's too early in our relationship for that sort of thing."

"I don't think I'll have time to go to that party. Besides, I really don't know anyone there."

"I know I don't like my boss. But going to another company would get me a boss I don't know. He could be worse."

"I have time for one last sales call. Let's see, I could call on my old buddy, John, or try that new company across the street. What the hell, I haven't seen John in weeks."

Some Causes

Because virtually all our fears center on the potential behavior of other people, is it any surprise that most of us fear meeting new people? When given the choice, even experienced salespeople would prefer to call on an old, familiar customer rather than knock on a strange door. This fear is a combination of our normal fears of people and the fear of the unknown, of meeting someone new and unpredictable. After all, new people may flirt with our significant other, laugh at us, criticize or confront us, or merely point out to everyone how "wimpy" we truly are.

We have learned that our old friends will not reject us—that's why they're our old friends. But strangers might do these things. Experience has taught us that our pal, Mary, will not criticize us, but strangers might. Many dates with Bill have led us to become comfortable with him. Bill has never confronted us about our beliefs; that's why we like him—but strangers might. As a result, we often miss out on meeting "Mr. Right"; comfort with the old is preferable to fear of the new.

A stranger could be warm, gracious, and complimentary. But that's of little significance to us. Why? Because we are not driven by what's good for us, but rather by what we fear. We do not love good, we merely fear being hurt. A love of good would lead us to be good, whereas our fear of potential danger merely leads us to be fearful. So even our love of good friends attending the party does not override our fear of the strangers who will also be there, and we refuse to go. Or we go to the party, hug the wall, and avoid interactions with strangers (at least until we've had enough wine).

Some Consequences

It is difficult to change someone's behavior. Our fear of meeting new people is one big reason. External forces (other people) are the major source of change in our lives. But if they're always the same people (or the same kinds of people) with whom we normally interact, change will not occur.

Who are these people? As we've seen, they are often the ones who share our fears. But these are the people who won't confront our fears, which is why we feel safe with them. Thus, we stay the same because we're comfortable only with the same kinds of people. Too often, we go through life seeking the same—the same types of friends, the same external forces to influence us.

More important, we avoid those who are different, those who might question and confront our fears, those who might show us more effective approaches to life and its problems. Although they may make us uncomfortable, these are often the very people who could help us most. They are the people who would question our fears, rather than share them. They could show us how unrealistic our fears are and how ineffective they make us. People who are "different" might make us uncomfortable, but only with respect to our fears. And we won't grow until we're uncomfortable with our fears.

Who does the depressed person seek out most often, a cheerful person or someone who shares their sadness? Who could help them most?

Who does the smothering person seek out, an independent, confident person or one who likes and reinforces their smothering?

Who does the person who fears criticism seek out, an open, forthright person or a passive, gentle person who also fears being criticized?

It's important to be aware of whether this fear is having an overly strong influence on us. If meeting new people makes us so uncomfortable that we excessively avoid interactions with more diverse people than we presently have in our inner circle, we have a fear that we would do well to address forcefully. The people who make us uncomfortable are sometimes the only ones who can broaden our response repertoire.

Excessive Behaviors

Did you ever tell your spouse you wanted to go to a party but he/she fought vigorously against it? Have you ever had someone close to you argue against inviting someone over because they might be boring or because "nobody knows them"? Have you ever suggested a dinner party only to have your significant other repeatedly criticize the idea as inappropriate when contrasted with watching "the game of the year"?

These are people who don't want to meet new people. The intense anger and defensiveness they show when confronted with the possibility of meeting new people (thus interrupting their football or work schedule) is proportional to their fear in this area.

More opportunities in life are probably lost because of the fear of meeting new people than any other. Why? Because, although our fears center on the behavior of others, it is also paradoxically true that most of the joys we derive from life come from other people. A wider genetic pool is advantageous for a species' survival. A wider response repertoire is advantageous for an individual facing life's challenges. And having a wide response range is often dependent on a wide range of friends. And this is often dependent on seeking out new and different people for our inner and even our "outer" circle (our pool of acquaintances).

To limit this pool because of our fear of meeting new people is often disastrous. Both vocational and personal success will depend, to a great extent, on the opportunities presented to us...by other people. Most opportunities, it's true, will be of little significance. But that's one reason we need a lot of opportunities presented to us if we are to find the few gems available in financial, vocational, personal, and every other area of our life.

Excessively Avoided Behavior

An exuberant emotional response when interacting with others? Shouts of glee over seeing old friends after years of separation? Spontaneous bursts of joy and laughter over common experiences a new acquaintance shares with you? Absence of such actions indicates that positive emotional responsiveness with people is not in this individual's repertoire. Why? Because joy when dealing with people, let alone strangers, is not felt by this person...fear is. This fear often rules out positive emotional responses to people. It's the same fear of people that leads many to be so bland, so "extinguishing" with people, and so fearful of meeting new ones.

Recluse. Hermit. Meeting new people is so aversive, so negative to some people that they adopt a lifestyle minimizing human interaction of any kind. They withdraw from environments that include people, environments that require interacting with others. People who fear meeting strangers lose many of the joys and benefits of human interaction. Their fear of meeting new people denies them a life filled with the rich variety of stimulation that only new people can provide. They become narrow and uninteresting. Want to alleviate boredom? Try meeting new people.

On occasion, we've all experienced fear of meeting new people. Our nervous stomach over a first date, our last-minute cancellation of a blind date or a speech—these are fairly common. But it is a fear that deprives us of more than we can ever imagine and, by definition, will ever know. Shyness is not merely an unpleasant phenomenon. Shyness is symptomatic of a destructive fear that almost ensures a barren, boring life.

People are most effective in situations they like, seek out, and enjoy. We might try consciously and deliberately to like, seek out, and enjoy meeting new people. We might try being emotionally expressive when meeting people. People can't help liking people who like them! Think of how many of your fears won't be confronted by these wonderful new people because they like you (and all because you like them).

If we take every opportunity we can to meet new people, we'll lead a much richer, more rewarding life. If we try to enthusiastically meet new people, enthusiastically like them, and express our liking for them, we might well end up a much sought-after, respected, and loved person. (How to reach this state is the subject of part II of this book.)

Summary

Can we:

1. Tell and discuss with a significant other how we feel some of their views are just plain wrong?

2. Go to a party alone when we know few people who will be there, start talking to a stranger on an elevator, or eagerly await the arrival of a blind date?

If we cannot do these things periodically and when appropriate, we might have a fear we'd do well to address. But we should not berate ourselves if we cannot do them. Other people influence us and we'll soon learn how we can get others to constructively help us change and grow.

Chapter Nine

13. Fear of Economic Deprivation

Can you say something like the following to your significant other (including your *most* significant other…yourself)? "I know the job means a lot more money, but I just didn't like the people there, so I said no."

This is certainly one of the most pervasive fears in our society, the **fear of economic deprivation.** The number of women who experience the vision of becoming financially destitute is startling. The number of men who fear economic deprivation (as evidenced by their fear of the financial responsibility of a family) is as great. Can we give up money and financial security for anything else? Or do we wear "golden hand-cuffs"? Do economic factors determine where we work, where we live, with whom we associate, whom we marry?

How many of us marry, in part, for economic security (or as much of it as we think marriage will get us)? The number would be staggering. Truth be told, it's more often from the female that fear of economic deprivation seeks its solution in marriage. But it is also a widespread fear in males (although in a different form), especially those raised by Depression Era parents or their children.

Some Causes

Before turning to the historical factors causing the fear of economic deprivation, it should be noted that money is an enormously powerful control factor in interpersonal relations. That is, having money gives a person a good deal of influence over others and can easily determine what they can expect and demand of people. Conversely, not having money often gives others a good deal of control over us, sometimes determining what we have to put up with from others. Indeed, few things give an individual more control over more people than having money. Why? Because so many people fear the lack of it. Thus, any discussion of the importance of the fear of economic deprivation must be viewed in the context of the pervasive fear of being controlled.

The Great Depression had an impact on everyone alive at that time. Our parents or grandparents spread the fears spawned by the Depression throughout society, an influence felt to the present day.

"How much did that cost?"
"You've got to save your money if you want to get ahead."
"People spend money so foolishly."
"That's just spending money without any regard for others."
"Why on earth would you spend so much for that?"
"I can't believe you were foolish enough to buy that."
"You really can't afford that."
"A penny saved is a penny earned."
"A fool and his money are soon parted."

How many relationships start, stop or continue because of the influence of economic factors? A great many. And the Depression had great influence on making economic factors so important in our attitudes toward economic deprivation. Also acting as reminders to reinforce fears in this area are the periodic recessions most countries go through.

What is the hallmark of capitalism? Competition! And competition is the absolute requirement for efficiency in any organization. But the stress competition can lead to in our efforts to survive economically can be considerable. And with the global competitive economy and the resulting intense focus on efficiency ("reengineering" and downsizing), the fear of economic deprivation is spreading rapidly. It is probably felt by more people and more intensely than ever before. The stress of competition influences many fears, such as fear of criticism, being seen as a failure, being disliked, and disappointing others (e.g., superiors).

Some Consequences

Because this is a book on fear, our focus is not on what money gives us, but on what the fear of lack of money burdens us with. While money allows us to influence, and even control others, the fear of lack of money often stems from our fear of being influenced, and even controlled (see next section) by others. Enormous amounts of behavior, both in and out of the work setting, are influenced by the fear of economic deprivation.

Excluding counterfeiters, money comes to us from only one source—other people. Because our fears center on the behavior of others, it is often our fears that prevent us from making more money. Consequently, if someone fears people, they often interact ineffectively with their only source of economic security (if there is such a thing). Thomas Watson, the builder of IBM, once said, "If my people don't like the customer, they don't get the order." Fully 90 percent of firings in the workplace occur, not because of a lack of technical competence, but because of a person's inability to get along with other people.

Conversely, few things give people the opportunity to make money through their own labor more than their liking and seeking out other people, new and different people, people outside their immediate world. As we've seen, the diversity of people in our inner circle broadens our behavior base and makes us more effective in responding to the different situations we encounter, especially in the work setting. This is one reason the fear of meeting new people can be so destructive, particularly in the arena of making money. We can be effective in our personal lives because *we* determine who we'll interact with, and those people we choose are usually quite similar. No such freedom is given us in the business setting, thus making our personal growth more likely there. Interacting with more diverse types of people, we are forced to broaden our response repertoire if we wish to reach our goals. Thus, the consequences of fearing economic deprivation, as with all fears, makes us less effective with people, making it more likely we'll be economically deprived.

Excessive Behavior

The "captains of industry," the intensely ambitious people who would rather "reign in hell than serve in heaven," can all be driven by the fear of being seen as a failure by others *or* by the fear of economic deprivation and the control others would have over them as a result.

The accumulation of positive reinforcers (money) often has little lasting impact on this fear (again, all reinforcers are transient alleviators of fear). The behavior of spending money, for example, if punished by Depression Era parents, leads to a fear of economic deprivation through excessive spending by the child. This is a fear that is not cured by the accumulation of wealth (despite rational theories of economics to the contrary). The stories of billionaires who require their guests to use a pay phone for personal calls or who are late for meetings because they were looking for a parking space in order to avoid paying a parking fee are legion. In effect, these people have learned *not* to spend money. They may have learned it when they didn't have money, but they didn't unlearn it when they did have money.

High-stake gamblers, for all the Freudian interpretations, are made adrenaline addicts more by their fear of economic deprivation, boredom—and the fear of being controlled by others—than by any sexual urges. The joy of actually winning is as short-lived as the fear of losing. What is permanent is the fear of economic deprivation. Without it, there would be no joy in gambling (in Las Vegas or in the stock market). But winning more than enough money to live out one's life in splendor rarely causes the investor (gambler) to pause. The fear lives!

For most of us, economic deprivation always looms on the horizon. The amount of money we have is irrelevant and hardly alleviates the fear at all. Why? Because achieving the goal of economic security has the same impact on our fear that any reinforcer has—its effects are transient and short-lived. Thus, many lives are spent striving for goals that, when attained, are found to be wanting. This may well eliminate the goal, but rarely the striving.

The salesperson who changes jobs fourteen times in nine years is often driven to make such sacrifices by a fear of economic deprivation. So is the young executive who jumps from one company to another, but always with a raise in salary. So is the workaholic who puts in too many late hours. The fear of economic deprivation, like all fears, gives others, especially their employers, a good amount of control over them.

What keeps many marriages together despite difficult conflicts between spouses? What keeps many children home with their parents long after they should have become independent? What keeps many people in dead-end jobs they hate? Fear of not having a job, i.e., fear of economic deprivation. What keeps most of us from taking realistic risks that could lead to a semblance of economic freedom? The same fear.

Why does Mary stay with an abusive husband? Sometimes it's fear of economic deprivation. Why is Sally so subservient to such a scorning, critical husband? Sometimes it's fear of economic deprivation. What are the two relevant issues in any divorce? Children (when appropriate)…but always money. Why? Same fear.

Excessively Avoided Behavior

Marriage is indeed one of the most prevalent **desires** of those who fear economic deprivation. But what is often assiduously avoided by those with this fear? Marriage. Who avoids marriage because of a fear of economic deprivation? The person who is expected to be the economic provider. A person with this fear often sees too many economic responsibilities associated with marriage. Watch the fear in the eyes of the provider when she or he is told that the discussions of having children have just been superseded by the reality of "pregnancy." Children have an enormous impact on a marriage, and economics is a major reason. Fear of economic deprivation also extends to the workplace. The number of people who work in large companies (or government agencies) in positions far below their capabilities is vast and is often the result of their fear of economic deprivation. For them, security is crucial; hence, they avoid going out on their own or even looking for a new job. This personal cautiousness often results from fear of economic deprivation.

Large organizations have often given a false sense of security to people fearing economic deprivation. Those who join large, prestigious companies are frequently told that the fear of being laid off is irrelevant, not a possibility. The arrogance of the "promise" often reflects itself in the management of the company. This same arrogance will ignore the needs of customers and eventually result in a precipitous drop in profits—and numerous layoffs.

14. Fear of Being Controlled

Can you make this statement to your significant other? "I'm kind of at a loss as to what to do here. Could you give me some help?"

Are you one of those legendary people who never ask for directions while you wander over the countryside? Are you fearful that someone will know you need them at times? Are you afraid of being seen as dependent? Are you **fearful of being controlled?**

Having this fear gives people great control over us. When someone does us a favor, we feel uneasy, uncomfortable, and try to repay them ten times over—anything to avoid being obligated to them. But it doesn't work. They did us a favor and now we're obligated to them; they have control over us (probably not in their mind, but certainly in ours, if we have this fear). So we resist letting people help us and do favors for us.

Some Causes

As we've seen, we "talk" in order to influence (control) the thinking and behavior of others. Most of this is done to prevent people from engaging in the behaviors we fear. Conversely, we tend to fear people who have control over us. After all, there may be little we can do to stop them from engaging in those dreaded behaviors. Thus, the fear of being controlled can be quite formidable.

Being controlled frequently involves coercion of some kind. This means that the person is being asked to do something they would rather not do. Many institutions, such as schools, rely heavily on some type of punishing control to achieve results. Ironically, children who have been ignored or given a good deal of independence by their parents will often rebel against the controlling influence.

As we've seen, the fear of being controlled is a big factor in the subconscious motivation of many people who avoid marriage. Dating exclusively for ten years does not elicit a proposal. Nagging ultimatums for marriage have the effect of driving a person with this fear away—far away.

How do we bring forth a proposal from someone who fears being controlled? By being very good to the person, doing them many favors, and asking nothing in return. Then quietly, without emotion, stating that's it's marriage or "I'll have to leave." No hysterics. This is not to be said as a threat because that will be seen as too controlling. Just a quiet statement of the facts. Then leave! Then hope the fear of being alone (and their guilt) takes precedence over their now dormant fear of being controlled by you (after all, you're gone). But you must leave the initiative to return (the control) to them! If they don't return, at least you're no longer wasting your time.

Some Consequences

One of the most destructive fears in the economic area is the fear of being controlled. Many excellent people have not been successful in making money because of this fear. This is commonly called an "authority problem." Their fear of being controlled makes them uncooperative, ineffective, and even destructive, with people above them. The fear of being controlled leads to an excessive sensitivity to being treated unfairly by others, but especially superiors. The resulting negative attitudes toward senior-level people virtually bar success in any organization. People who fear being controlled usually have failing careers unless they become entrepreneurs (even that doesn't ensure success, because customers are always the "boss" to an effective entrepreneur).

Managing others, however, is a different story for those with this fear. How many supervisors find themselves doing their subordinates' work. Why? Because the manager's fear of being controlled, even by his/her own subordinates, causes them to do most of the work themselves. "It was easier to do it myself than explain it all to him." So while the employees play golf on Saturday, the boss works her heart out, putting in long hours to get the job done. Now who has control? And who bears the weight of responsibility?

Why do some couples live together in harmony for years, but after marriage, break up? Sometimes it's because one fears being controlled, and marriage is one of the great symbols of control. It represents the state's right to set standards and determine certain obligations. And the state will exact a price if you want out of the marriage. Now that's control.

If someone is able to get another who fears being controlled through the engagement process, the marriage itself can prove traumatic and full of argumentative interchanges. This is due, in some part, to marriage making the person even more sensitive to being controlled. Situations that had been acceptable are now cause for argument. Do we want our spouse to go to a play, an art exhibit? Suddenly, we're trying to control him. Do we want our spouse to call us when he'll be home late? He reacts more negatively—because we're trying to control him. Do we want our spouse to occasionally have friends join us for drinks? He seems quicker to anger over our request, partially because we're trying to control him.

Now, it should be noted that our spouse will often give plausible reasons for not doing the things we request. He will readily associate our suggestions with *realistic* negatives. "The people at those art exhibits are phoney," or "Your friends don't really want to see me." Good associations. Reasonable. Why do they come to his mind, and why are they so important to him? Because he fears being controlled.

Being married to someone who fears being controlled is difficult at best. If we don't like what they do and criticize them, they feel frustrated and angry. Why? Because we're trying to control them by criticizing them (which, indeed, we are; but that's a fact that merely makes us part of the human race). If we like something that they don't like, they often feel frustrated and angry. Why? Because we're trying to control them when we speak favorably of the things we like.

Excessive Behaviors

The people who excessively fear inability to control (fear it even more than most of us) often do so because they really fear *being controlled*. They go out of their way to control people so people won't have a chance to control them. These people truly dominate interpersonal relationships. They talk too much and listen too little. They want to influence others rather than patiently taking the time to evaluate situations and people so that their attempts at influencing are more effective and productive.

The entrepreneur loves the joy of independence? Not necessarily. He often is driven by the fear of dependence. Why? Because it gives the person he is dependent on too much control over him.

The confirmed bachelor (he's 35 and never married) loves the free and easy lifestyle? Not necessarily. He often fears the terror of commitment. Why? Because it can give the person he is committed to an awful lot of influence over him.

Then there is the insensitive clod who always forgets birthdays, is late for dates, and has no time for activities that he doesn't like but demands that others make time for things he does like. Is he a truly confident person who doesn't care what others think of him? Not necessarily. He may merely fear the idea of being controlled by others.

Excessively Avoided Behavior

Have you ever met a person with whom you just couldn't connect? They were superficially pleasant enough, but seemed to have little feeling over anything, any person, issue or thing. This avoidance of emotional involvement is often a way of preventing anyone from controlling them. People who fear being controlled usually lead solitary lives, free of any close relationships that could lead to being controlled by others.

Persons of this type are often difficult to fathom, since so little in life seems to interest them. They are loners because they fear the presence of anyone or anything being close or important to them, since it would then have the power to influence them. Their fear of being controlled leads them to withdraw, emotionally (intimacy) and even physically, from the most important thing that influences people—other people. Thus, they have really withdrawn from life itself. They are often the great "extinguishers" of our lives. They allow themselves an emotional investment in no one.

Summary

Our fears will reside in those areas in which we hesitate to:

1. Give up financial rewards when the true "price" we pay to get the financial rewards makes it an unreasonable bargain.

2. Look to others for help, guidance, and expertise when needed. Have the patience to evaluate others and allow others the freedom to be who they are and do what they want to do. Be flexible enough to adapt to the desires of others periodically.

Addendum

As we shall see, a main tenet of this book, in many ways the main tenet, is that people have a good deal of influence over us. A prominent fear in many people is that of being controlled. That makes one of the major premises of this book unpalatable to many people.

But, one might ask, suppose someone imposes their own fears on us when trying to influence us? Actually, those in our "inner circle" do just that; the fears of anyone close to us will always be visited upon us in one way or another. Indeed, any long-term relationship between two people will eventually be determined by the fears of the people involved and how those fears mesh or conflict.

Suppose our significant other fears being criticized or ridiculed by friends because of who their date is and what they look like. They'll watch everything we do, to the smallest detail. They'll become easily irritated over a hair out of place or a skirt that's "too short." In sum, they'll become overly critical of us and any shortcoming we have. Their fears will be visited upon us; they will influence us, one way or another.

Chapter Ten

15. Fear of Being the Center of Attention (Shyness)

Can you say the following to a significant other? "They asked me to give a talk at our next club meeting. I was elated."

If you find this difficult, you may be shy; you may **fear being the center of attention.** Why? Do you have doubts about yourself? Do you feel less than capable? If so, you're a member of a big club.

Some Causes

People who fear being the center of attention have often been punished, criticized, and ridiculed. As a result, they don't like themselves (an unfortunately common phenomenon). This can only increase their desire to avoid being the center of attention. Remember those early school years when we'd do almost anything to avoid being the center of attention, especially in front of our classmates? That's because children are often spontaneous—and often critical, particularly of those who get the attention of others, especially adults. Woe to the student who was singled out for praise by the teacher in front of the entire class. That student would often be singled out for ridicule at recess by his/her peers.

As a result, being the center of attention often means negative experiences in early years when our views of life and people are being formed. It is then that we are supposed to be conforming, to be following the rules and blending in with the group. Anyone who has been in the military and has been subjected to the threats and harassment of a drill instructor knows the pain of being singled out, of being the center of attention. They also know the diminished fear they feel (hence the reinforcing value) when someone else is the target for the dreaded punitive and harsh reprimands.

Giving a speech is often listed as one of the greatest fears many people experience in their lives. Self-consciousness is a prevalent phenomenon. It sometimes stems not from overt ridicule or insults, but from the unknown—not knowing what these people looking at us really think of us while we're giving this much-practiced speech. When we give a half-hour speech, we talk for an eternity (a half hour) and we haven't the slightest idea what anyone "out there" is feeling about us. There's no feedback. We're in a vacuum. Yet we have to keep talking. It's not a relaxed picture. And if we start our speech with a few jokes that no one laughs at, we'll know what "extinction" and true terror really are.

As we have seen, our fears center on the behavior of others. What people think of us is truly the basis of all fears, because it forms the precursor of any of our specific fears. Actually being disliked, seen to be insignificant or rejected occur or do not occur because of what others think of us. If we don't like ourselves, we're pretty sure no one else will. In our mind, this would almost guarantee bad experiences if we became the center of attention.

"Friends" often confront, punish, and ridicule shy people for being so "stupid" as to fear being the center of attention. In their desire to help, friends often point to the negative consequences of shyness. Their arguments are reasonable, logical, and rational. But these arguments are also destructive, especially since they are often motivated by the frustration experienced by the friends. This frustration leads to an anger and criticism that only makes the problem worse because it increases the shy person's dislike of themselves; it further detracts from their self-confidence.

Some Consequences

People who fear being the center of attention are exquisitely sensitive to criticism. Not liking themselves leaves them vulnerable to the feedback all of us need if we're to continue growing. Because criticism comes only from people, they fear people, especially unfamiliar people (since they might criticize them).

But, as we've seen, meeting new people (even critical ones) is essential for broadening our response range, for making us more effective in life. Consequently, shy people have an overly narrow response inventory. Their withdrawal from meeting diverse people is matched by their avoidance of rich, diverse behaviors. While it is often true that shy people have a rich fantasy life, this offers little comfort in a world so dependent upon interpersonal relations for the basic rewards of life.

Many individuals are drawn to shy people as life partners. This is often due to the individual's need to control and dominate others and/or the insecurity felt when a significant other interacts constructively with other people. In one extreme example, a dominating husband would censor the newspaper every day, cutting out articles he felt that his wife should not read. Her shyness prevented her from interacting with people who might influence her thinking along more constructive, proactive lines. Shy people, however, can be rather boring to live with if they aren't alleviating some chronic fear of their partner; their narrow response repertoire prevents them from being more stimulating individuals.

Excessive Behavior

Many shy people frequently interact with inanimate objects rather than people; they have a "still-life mentality." They are much more comfortable reading, watching TV, and so forth. With the advent of the computer, man-machine relationships have taken on a new dimension. People who are shy and retiring in the presence of others can become quite aggressive when interacting with a computer. Indeed, many of the more brilliant and aggressive successes in the computer industry are shy and retiring individuals ("nerds"). They find confidence with a machine because it does not try to judge them or have the potential to do them the harm that people do.

And with the computer come the computer clubs, the chat groups (the "best sellers" of the internet). These provide the vehicles for people to interact with one another—but only via a machine and a modem. Thus, loneliness is alleviated through "social" interactions, but without anyone actually seeing or even hearing anyone else. And because stopping an interaction merely requires hitting a switch, few people could ever criticize or threaten the shy person. Getting "bad" people out of one's computer life is relatively easy, requiring minimal confrontation.

Because of their need to avoid the spotlight, shy people are normally good listeners. This trait is enhanced by the fact that they rarely like themselves, hence the lives of others are more interesting to them. This can make them attractive companions, especially to those who need a lot of attention. Because they avoid people, they also develop strong loyalties to the few friends they have. Thus, their friends rarely experience competition for their attention.

Excessively Avoided Behavior

Shy, placating, "perfect" employees are engaged in an avoidance of any activities that might lead others to focus attention on them. Shy people follow orders and regulations closely, adhere rigidly to social strictures, and even dress blandly. Shy people do not want to do anything that makes them seem different, unique, or stand out from others. This means that they are overly monotone, rarely showing any emotion. And without emotional expressiveness, their impact on others is minimal. Thus, they are too easily taken advantage of, avoiding the attention that confrontations would involve.

Shy people adhere closely to the socially proper way of doing things. They blend in. Shy people are usually model citizens and employees. They are hardly noticed, and that, after all, is their goal. These are safe, predictable, but often boring people. Shy people rigidly adhere to the covenants of any organization, making them passive to the point of being automatons. They look with bewilderment, awe, and fear at those who "march to a different drummer," those iconoclasts who will do anything to be the center of attention (and who often account for the progress of an organization). As a result, shy people rarely make a significant contribution to an organization. They often dread and avoid those who need to be seen as unique and different from the "masses."

The Conflicts of Shy Significant Others

Whereas we often seek out those who *share* our fears as friends, we definitely avoid those who would make us confront our fears. But this is not true of lovers and significant others. We seek out as partners those whom we expect to *lessen* our fears. Those who have our fears do not normally want to alleviate them. Thus, lovers cannot share our fears. Because they do not have our fears, we see them as confident.

We don't see, however, that our lovers have their own fears. We don't see this because we are so wrapped up in **our** own fears. Besides, we don't have their fear, so it doesn't even bother us. But after we're married and interact with them frequently and intimately, we'll see their fears. They'll be imposed on us and either frustrate us or be added to our own. And vice versa! Then the frustration caused by their fears will anger us. Why? Because their fear is stupid and silly. Why do we feel that way? Because we don't have that fear.

A politician, for example, often fears being insignificant to people. He's comfortable and stimulated, therefore, only when interacting with people, being in the limelight and "pressing the flesh." It's what makes him successful. It's his joy in life. But suppose his wife is shy and fears being in the limelight. His wife is awed by his confidence. Why does she see him as so confident? Because he doesn't have her fear of being the center of attention.

This salesman fears being alone. He has, as a result, great initiative to go out and interact with people. And it helps make him successful. His wife is shy and fears meeting new people. She married her husband precisely because he's confident, meaning only that he doesn't have her fear in this area.

Why did each of these couples marry? Because they were awed by their spouse's confidence. They thought their spouse was confident because their spouse didn't have their fear. (And the politician and salesman initially see their spouse as confident because they don't have an insatiable need for attention.) Each person was so involved in their own fear, they didn't see their fiance had fears of their own, because they were different fears. But the politician or sales person may be quite successful. This may lead them to feel that their shy spouse is a liability to them. The resulting frustration is often communicated (subtly or not) and, as a result, the shy spouse's guilt and dislike of herself increases, thus leading to more fear of attention and more withdrawal from people. Thus, the marriage sinks deeper into problems that might well lead to extramarital affairs or alcoholism or divorce.

16. Fear of Boredom

Can you say this to a significant other? "You know, we've gone to the same cottage on the same island for our vacation every year. You'd think we'd be tired of it, but I look forward to it all year. I really love it there."

Can you say this? If not, you may have one of the most underrated, ignored, and pervasive of all human phenomena—the **fear of boredom**.

The fear of boredom is not the same as boredom itself, just as the fear of being seen as a failure is not the same as failure itself. Fear is often an anticipatory response, a reaction to something that isn't presently happening. But because it might happen at any time, fear is on guard all the time, hence it leads to exaggerated and inappropriate behavior.

We try a three-day cruise. We're bored. We don't go on any more cruises. That's appropriate. That's a constructive, realistic reaction based on experience. It's not fear.

We've never been on a cruise. We refuse to go on a three-day cruise because we fear we'd be bored. But we'll never know if we would enjoy it…because we'll never do it. We're reacting without experience or knowledge. That's inappropriate. We're reacting irrationally and inappropriately (especially if our significant other wants to go on a cruise). Our reactions are being driven by our fear, our anticipation that things will go badly.

Some Causes

People who fear boredom are normally aggressive and proactive. They have a great deal of initiative, take chances, and readily enter new and unfamiliar areas. People who fear boredom are quick to engage in activities that will achieve their goals successfully, even if their success is only momentary. What are their goals? The same as everyone else's—to lessen their fears. But what actually bores them? Any activities that do not alleviate their other fears.

If, for example, they fear being insignificant to people, they may have found that playing the lead role in their high school play alleviated that fear. They may have then turned to the risky profession of acting and/or show business generally. "Working in an office is too predictable, too boring."

If they fear economic deprivation, they turn to commodity or investment speculation. Here the action is constant and the potential for lessening their fear of economic deprivation almost always present. They avoid being "one of the masses" and working in areas in which their ability to diminish their fear is too predictable and dependent on a monthly paycheck.

If they fear being controlled by others (and many do because "people can be so boring"), they may become entrepreneurs—over and over again, despite repeated failures. "Working for a corporation, with all its restrictive rules, would be terribly smothering of my creative thought processes!"

Some Consequences

Because a person who fears boredom reacts excessively, they anticipate being bored. Hence, they are *always* looking for something new and different, and this includes new people. Unlike most people who react to a first date with anxiety, their first date with a person is usually their best. This is when they show the most interest in the other person because they're new and unknown. But their interest wanes rapidly on subsequent dates, a phenomenon their companion is at a loss to understand.

Trying to build a long-term, intimate relationship with an individual who fears boredom is virtually impossible. Those who fear boredom are just too difficult to hold onto because absolutely no one can keep changing enough to "surprise" them, to continually stimulate them. No one can hold their interest, not even confident people with their wide response repertoire.

Excessive Behaviors

Too often, those who fear boredom engage in activities that are self-destructive because they fear they'll be bored. Watch an inveterate gambler. The need for "action" often supersedes better judgment. A professional gambler who doesn't fear boredom knows there are many times the best bet is no bet at all. The person who fears boredom, however, can't stand the lack of action. That is when they place poor bets and lose their money. Their fear of economic deprivation or failure is superseded by their fear of boredom. So they often lose.

Every job and every relationship contains within it the seeds of boredom. The president of the United States sometimes has to meet with presidents of various associations, a somewhat boring prospect at best. But every new relationship starts out to be interesting, if only for a few minutes. However, repetition of such meetings brings on predictability, similarity of behaviors, familiarity, hence periodic boredom. These natural episodes of boredom are readily adapted to by the normal person, but they can trigger excessive negative reactions by those who fear boredom.

People who fear boredom are not only risk-oriented and highly self-centered, they are also intensely emotional. These things can make them exciting to be with. Their unpredictability, and their constant need for change and stimulating activities, makes life with them a whirlwind for their companion. This quickly lessens most people's realistically (not fear-driven) negative reaction to some of the boredom inherent in much of life. As a result, people who fear boredom are often quite popular and sought-after during their single years. But great lovers don't necessarily make great spouses or even good, loyal friends.

Excessively Avoided Behavior

What is avoided is any interaction that doesn't continually lessen one of their fears. Because relationships rarely alleviate any of their fears, long-term stability with them is unlikely. Thus, dice and cards are often capable of doing what few people can: maintain the interest of these individuals. Patience and stability are not part of their repertoire. They love people, but only new and "fresh" people. Anyone committed to a person who fears boredom is virtually destined to be a failure in the relationship. As a result, interactions with those who fear boredom frequently compromise the other person's confidence.

Also avoided are passivity and dependency. Giving some control or influence to someone is incompatible with the person who fears boredom. Because those who fear boredom don't fear the unknown, as most of us do, they know that nobody will stimulate them (alleviate their fear) as well as they do themselves. This is one of the reasons underlying their self-centeredness and inability to focus on others.

Boredom is a strong motivator in life, even to people who don't have a fear of it. The fear of boredom makes the aversion much stronger and the behavior stemming from the fear excessive and inappropriate. Over the long term, few of us could satisfy those who fear boredom. If we're looking for some influence and some stability in a relationship, we might try to resist the initial excitement of being with the person who fears boredom. In the long term, most of us will bore them; thus, we'll be of little lasting significance to them, no matter how good and wonderful we are.

Summary

Our fears will reside in those areas in which we hesitate to:

1. Put ourself in situations in which the rewards could be rather worthwhile if we made a presentation or took responsibility for maintaining the interest of a group of people.

2. Allow ourself to become involved in some activities we've never tried because of prejudices we hold about the possibility of boredom, or hesitating to allow ourself periodic down time from the constant "adrenaline highs" of action, or failing to look for and find stability in our relationships.

Part II

Evaluating Other People
and Their Influence on Us

There's nothing I'm afraid of like scared people.

Robert Frost

Nothing in life is to be feared. It is only to be understood.

Marie Curie

Chapter Eleven

Who's In Charge Here?

We are taught to focus on ourselves, to take responsibility for our own actions, to be the captain of our own soul. To what end? So we can constructively change ourselves when it's deemed appropriate—by other people.

Where Do My Attitudes and Feelings Come From?

Few people would deny that *other people* have a good deal of influence over our thoughts, attitudes, feelings and behavior. So those who tell us that we can change ourselves may be leading us to a world of increased frustration and more failure. They're giving us a responsibility that's virtually impossible to carry out effectively if others are, indeed, influential in our lives. The result will be even more frustration and less confidence in ourselves and our capabilities.

What about the influence others have on us? Shouldn't we focus on that? It might be a good idea if we concerned ourselves with how people in our inner circle are affecting us, what they are doing to our confidence, our fears, our attitudes toward ourselves and other people, our work, and even our play. After all, people frequently remind us of the impact we have on them, especially when they feel that the impact is negative. We might as well focus periodically on what they do to us.

Linda doesn't actually look forward to her weekly dinners with Janice. It's nothing she can put her finger on. Linda just knows that she feels more irritable for about 24 hours after the dinners. Linda's boyfriend brought it to her attention, suggesting they not see each other after these Janice get-togethers because of Linda's negative, critical attitudes; he referred to it as Linda's weekly "PMS." Linda had known Janice since childhood and felt she couldn't end the relationship. She had discussed her irritability on numerous occasions with her psychiatrist, but to no avail.

What neither Linda nor her psychiatrist addressed was Janice, who she was, what she wanted from Linda, and how she went about getting it. As a result, Janice, and her effect on Linda, remained a mystery. No one, consequently, realized how much Janice feared the happiness of other people and how she subtly, but pervasively, punished it.

Do you know what is probably the most proven law in science? The law of inertia, which says that *any object (person) in the universe remains in its present state unless acted upon by external forces.* And what are the most important external forces acting on us? Other people!

So it is proper to concern ourselves at least occasionally with other people in our lives, who they are, and what influence they're having on us. This is especially true of those in our inner circle. It is the fears of those with whom we interact frequently and continually, those whom we seek out, like and love, and those who often seek out and interact with us, that will affect us the most.

Not focusing on the fears of other people can leave us unaware of what people are doing to us and to our feelings and attitudes about everyone and everything around us, including ourselves. We'll wonder where our fears came from and how we'll get rid of them. Determining the fears of the people in our inner circle and how they influence our own fears, ideas, hopes, and frustrations is one of the most personally profitable, confidence-building activities we can engage in. It is an effort that will reward us many times over.

The Frustration from a Lack of Awareness

The alternative is to be unaware of why we feel the way we do. We become sad and don't know why. We become frustrated and angry for no apparent reason. We grow uneasy with certain people whom we think we should like and feel guilty when we don't. We experience too much anxiety anticipating situations in which we have already done well and know we will probably continue to do well.

All these feelings make us feel worse about ourselves because we can't seem to determine where they came from and why they're so strong. And that leads to more self-doubt and more destructive self-criticism. As the self-doubt and self-criticism increase, we start to engage in behaviors that become excessive because they are fear-driven.

Anne is frequently depressed. She sleeps poorly, eats little, and is too often self-deprecating and withdrawn. Despite her physical attractiveness, her relations with men are short-lived. Sympathetic friends show their concern by advising Anne to "look on the bright side of things" while less patient friends admonish her to "stop feeling sorry for yourself." Neither approach does much good. People who are intimate with Anne's family are bewildered by her depression. Her family has always been loving and supportive. And Anne reciprocates, talking to her mother everyday and taking her parents to dinner most Sundays.

Few people, least of all Anne, would suspect that it's the interactions with her mother that caused, and are maintaining, Anne's depression. There are two reasons these suspicions would not arise. First, Anne's mother is known by everyone to be a "sweet, caring" person. Second, the depression is seen as Anne's problem and "only she can solve it."

One of the major tenets of this book is that Anne cannot solve the problem. Her depression is the result of outside influences, especially that of her mother. But confronting Anne with this idea probably would be futile. Not only would the idea be argued against by her mother, but Anne herself would have difficulty accepting the suggestion that someone so loving and dear to her was causing so much pain. Indeed, both mother and daughter would have trouble with the concept that other people had so much influence on their feelings.

This will be one of the most emotionally difficult suggestions in this book—the suggestion to focus on others and the influence they exert. The typical approach most of us take is to focus on how we can influence others to think better of us and to prevent them from criticizing, disliking, or rejecting us. This gives others a great deal of control over us and leaves us without a prayer of changing anything, especially ourselves and our happiness.

The ability to accept the necessity of **accurately evaluating** the people in our inner circle—and the **influence** they have on us—will provide us with some of the most powerful tools with which a person can go through life.

Know Thyself

Does self-knowledge change us? We'd love to think that we could change ourselves if we really knew who we were because it would give us control of ourselves and free us from the influence of others. True or false? False.

Know other people—they are the principal external forces acting on us. They are the forces that figure so prominently in our happiness or sadness, our passivity or our aggressiveness, our enthusiasm or our criticalness, our fear or our confidence.

We are an external force acting on them—and we can influence others! Mary and John sent their 12-year-old, overly rebellious son to a "sensitivity" camp and a highly competent psychologist. The psychologist "cured" the child and sent him home, whereupon he immediately reverted to his old rebellious behavior. Why? Because he went back to the same behavioral environment, the same external forces: his parents.

If the psychologist had changed the parents, she probably would have changed their son without ever having seen the boy.

It may seem hard to accept the idea that we frequently lack control and influence over ourselves. But accepting the idea that other people sometimes influence us is good enough. With that assumption, few people should argue the point that determining who other people are and how they do influence us is an important consideration in our lives.

But I Am Who I Am!

Why is our behavior so stable? Because we continue to seek out the same kinds of people as friends, principally those who **share** our fears. Thus, the behaviors around us, and the people (external forces) acting on us, remain the same. Worse, we tend to avoid those who don't have our fears. Why? Because they might confront them or engage in the very behaviors that frighten us so.

The overly sensitive person gathers people about her who share her fear of criticism and confrontation, since they are least likely to criticize or confront her. The depressed person tends to seek out sad individuals while avoiding cheerful people, often referring to the latter in negative ways ("naive, Pollyannas"). The "macho" man seeks out those who share his interest in rugged sports; that is, people who share his fear of being seen as frightened or weak by others.

The Most Effective Focus

Our fears are usually too great to allow us to focus on accurately evaluating people around us. We want to influence them. But to what end? To make sure they don't engage in any behaviors that might threaten us. This is a sad mistake. How can we possibly change and grow when so many of our interactions and so much of our effort is centered on merely preventing some behaviors in others?

Let's try a different road, periodically at least. Let's concentrate on finding people who are good for us! How? By first evaluating *everyone* with whom we interact on a regular basis, especially those in our inner circle. We'll soon realize that it is often *their fears* that will determine what we feel, the joy we get from life, the pain we try to avoid, our happiness, our sadness, our success or failure. In sum, we'll find that the fears of those in our inner circle are infectious.

Let's forget our pride and "independence" for a moment. People influence us, our thinking and attitudes. Let's stop wondering what others think of us and focus on what we think of them and the impact they have on us.

Summary

Too often, we focus on effects rather than causes. Focusing on our feelings and attitudes is a case in point. Our feelings are an effect, a consequence. The causes of our feelings often lie not in ourselves and under our control, but in the behavior of those with whom we interact frequently and repetitively.

It is important to focus on the behavior of those in our "inner circle" and the influence their behavior has on us and our feelings and attitudes.

Introspection and "knowing thyself" are interesting and sometimes helpful endeavors. But they rarely *change* anyone. Many people know they are indecisive or too critical and are unable to do anything about it. That's partially because they're focused on themselves and the effects others have had on them.

Let's focus on causes, the external forces influencing us. Because of our own fears, we "sit back" and evaluate people's impact on us too rarely. Instead, we spend too much time blindly trying to influence others in our unsuccessful attempts to alleviate *our own fears*. Constantly evaluating the people around us (to which we now turn) and their impact on us is a major key to opening the doors to **self-confidence**.

People influence us differently, each in an individual way. And the effects they have on us are crucial; they go a long way toward making us who we are. Know thyself? No. Know others. Know those in our inner circle, those who have so much influence over us.

So let's find out who these people truly are in our inner circle. We'll be in a much better position not only to understand them and what they're doing to us, but also to know how to influence them most effectively. And our efforts to influence them, if we've taken the time to understand them, will be that much more effective. But, most important, we'll be aware of the impact they have on our most treasured asset, our self-confidence.

Chapter Twelve

Who Are Our Friends?

Evaluating or Influencing

There are two basic paths or orientations to take when interacting with people: we can *evaluate* them or we can try to *influence* them. Virtually all of us focus almost exclusively on influencing them. And therein lies the source of many of our difficulties in life.

When we patiently take the time to assess people, our attempts to influence them will be much more effective and successful. Knowing, for example, which of the sixteen behaviors discussed in previous chapters our significant other has difficulty engaging in can provide invaluable insights. This knowledge can tell us who they are and what they are capable or incapable of becoming. It will tell us what they like and what they fear. Most important, it will tell us what their impact on us will be, what they will want us to become over the long term. Thus, patiently evaluating people in our inner circle should tend to make our expectations of the relationship more realistic, and help us determine if we even want a relationship with this person.

Objectivity

We don't evaluate people every waking moment, of course—just occasionally. When is occasionally? When we want to. There is one exception to "when we want to." We should never evaluate someone when we're angry. Yet it's when we're angry that we're usually most motivated to do an assessment and give people our "helpful" suggestions.

Evaluating someone when we're angry makes our evaluations unrealistic and readily leads us to make poor decisions and take destructive actions. The only time to evaluate anyone is when everything is going well; that is, when we're most likely to see their "normal" behavior— their frequent, repetitive behavior.

But we don't have to let people know we're evaluating them. Our old motto: They act, we feel and react! Our new motto: They do, we evaluate, we think, we use our mind...then we allow ourselves the luxury of feeling and reacting. And because we *think* first, our *feelings* will be more understanding, calm, and compassionate—and our behavior with them more effective.

To evaluate someone accurately means that we will try to *avoid* thinking of people in terms of: 1) who we want them to be, 2) who they think they are, 3) who they want us to think they are, and (especially) 4) who other people tell us they are.

It should also be noted that evaluating people will help free us from the old trap of treating everyone the same. We'll be more discriminating in our relationships. We'll be more inclined toward seeing the differences in people, the uniqueness of each person. Then we'll be less inclined toward making the same old mistakes with every new significant other in our lives. The "baggage" all of us carry into new relationships will be minimal.

A Quick and Effective Insight into People

There is a quick and effective way of evaluating people, a method that is most appropriate for the impatient among us. People can respond in one of three ways to someone's (our) behavior: 1) They can respond positively, especially in an emotional manner (reinforcement); 2) they can respond neutrally, in a monotonic way (extinction), or 3) they can respond negatively, in a critical way (punishment).

If they respond positively and reinforce the other person, it means they *like* the behavior the other person just engaged in and want to strengthen it (increase its frequency). Further interactions with an individual who emotionally reinforces specific behaviors in others will do just that, strengthen that particular behavior.

If an individual responds neutrally and extinguishes certain behaviors in others, it means they *don't care* one way or the other about the behavior, or they *dislike* the behavior of the person. This extinction will weaken the person's behavior.

And if an individual responds negatively and punishes the person, it simply means they *don't like* the person's current behavior. Thus, they want to stop this particular behavior in the person. (And if the person continues to interact with the individual, they probably will stop it.)

So if a person responds positively to what we're doing at the moment, we'll know they like this behavior and want us to act this way more often. If they respond neutrally, we'll know they either don't care or dislike this behavior. And if they respond negatively, we'll know they dislike our behavior of the moment.

Then we'll know what they really like or don't like in us (despite what they might say to the contrary). Someone might say they're elated over our promotion, for example, but react in a neutral (extinguishing) or even negative (punishing) way when we tell them the "good news." This reaction is a far more accurate guide as to how they truly feel.

This will also tell us what influence our friends will have on us, what feelings and attitudes they'll instill or strengthen, and which they'll weaken in us over the long term. To find out what behaviors our friends like and dislike in us, therefore, all we need do is "throw out" some behavior and note in which of the three ways our friends respond to what we do.

Let's look at the three reactions in reverse order, starting with punishment and then extinction. We'll save positive reinforcement for the next chapter.

Negative Response: Punishment

Let's see if our friends like us "being in love" with someone. We'll say, "You know, Brad and I really get along well. He's such a thoughtful, considerate guy. I've been thinking of dating him." We'll say this enthusiastically. Our minds will be active, however, for we'll be watching the reaction of our "friend" closely and objectively. Despite our comment about Brad, we will *not* be thinking about Brad; our focus will be on the person to whom we're talking. In sum, we will be *thinking* instead of *feeling*, evaluating instead of trying to influence. Rather than showing our normal concern over what this person thinks of us, we'll be considering what we think of this person's reactions to our feelings about Brad. Then we'll consider what influence those kinds of reactions are likely to have on us over the long term.

The first person we say this to, Mary, responds, "I really can't believe you're that naive. Brad is such a wimp! Everyone knows that!"

Mary responded negatively. She punished us. Does this mean that Mary doesn't like our relationship with Brad? *Yes*, especially if she responds in a consistently negative way to any additional positive, enthusiastic comments we make about Brad. As we shall see, we will judge people only by their frequent, repetitive behavior, not by a single instance or by one isolated reaction.

Frequent, Repetitive Behavior Is the Mark of a Person

We may well want to mention some positive things about Brad to Mary two or three times over the next few days just to make sure of our evaluation, especially if her response surprised us and seems out of character for her. But we will not argue with her. We accept and respect any response she makes because we want a spontaneous reaction from her, now and subsequently. We're evaluating, not trying to influence Mary at this moment, so we're "nonjudgmental."

If we truly like Brad (or anyone else for that matter), should we talk about them with anyone who punishes our positive, enthusiastic attitudes? No! If our "friend" subsequently punishes our expressions of enthusiasm about others (Jim and Bill), then interacting with our "friend" will gradually weaken our positive feelings toward others. The thought that we can overcome their influence on our feelings is dangerous. Their impact will always instill some doubt, some hesitancy in us. This hesitancy will show itself in the relationship and further erode it. For example, if our parents punished our enthusiasm or affection for people throughout our childhood, we might have some difficulty building close, intimate relationships now.

Marital Relationships

This is not, incidentally, an unusual situation for marital partners. Many people are threatened by their spouse's respect, admiration, or enthusiasm for another person, especially someone of the opposite sex. Feeling threatened by the possibility of being insignificant or lacking the influence of others over their spouse, they frequently—but subtly—punish their spouse's positive feelings for others. This leads to tension in the relationship at best and isolation from other people at worst. If both do it to each other, it can lead to rather severe social withdrawal by the couple.

Continually being punished (even subtly) for positive and enthusiastic feelings for anyone else (this is true "smothering" behavior) can have a devastating impact on a person. We should always be alert to anyone with this fear being in our inner circle.

Neutral Response: Extinction

Let's turn to another friend, Ann. We again enthusiastically say, "You know, Ann, Brad and I really get along well. He's such a thoughtful, considerate guy. I've been thinking of dating him."

Ann, in a perfunctory manner, responds, "That's good. Say listen, are we still going to that movie Friday night?" Ann did not respond emotionally to our behavior; to many people (probably including us), that's extinction!

In sum, Ann has responded neutrally. She doesn't like our admiration of Brad. She may not care or she may dislike it; only further "tests" will tell. But we do know that she doesn't like it (despite her protests to the contrary, if we foolishly accuse her). And Ann's neutral reaction will have an enormous impact on us.

Any neutral reaction by someone instills anger and/or fear in the person toward whom it was directed. A neutral reaction is probably the most common response people use when dealing with others.

> *Wife* (excitedly): I won the tennis championship at the club today!
> *Husband*: How many were in the tournament?

Can the wife feel anything but frustration and anger over her husband's bland reaction? Should we wonder why she "snipes" at him on subsequent occasions, when we know he's a non-responsive, non-expressive, extinguishing person?

It is quite possible that some people, such as Ann and the husband, learned in childhood that responding neutrally is the safest way to react to anyone under any circumstance. We may find that these monotonic, non-expressive people were punished for displaying any emotion, affection, or enthusiasm by rigid, constrictive parents. And our insights may lead us to be quite sympathetic toward them.

Should Sympathy Inspire Love?

In terms of **our** well-being, however, it doesn't matter how they got that way or what their parents did to them! Their bland reaction to enthusiasm in others means they're uncomfortable with positive feelings expressed by others. This may be especially apparent when our positive feelings center on other people or situations with which the "extinguishers" have no involvement. And their pervasively bland reactions to our enthusiasm will be contagious if they are in our inner circle. They will wear down our enthusiasm and we will be infected.

Frequent interactions with bland, "extinguishing" people will not only kill our enthusiasm, but will initially increase our frustration and anger. We will eventually become lethargic ourselves, devoid of feelings (except an underlying anger and fear). These people will make us one of them, regardless of how they got that way. This lethargy is frequently apparent in workplace departments that are managed by bland, monotonic, extinguishing people. Sympathy should play no part in our *objective evaluations* of people and their impact on us.

Yet too often, these extinguishing people are the very people we strive after. Why? Because we misinterpret their constant neutral reactions and general blandness as signs of confidence or as an intriguing mysteriousness. After all, they're obviously not quaking in their boots as we are. We express feelings—hate, love, enthusiasm—and they don't seem to care. No one can sway them. How independent they are! How confident they must be that nothing fazes them! If only I could be like that!

We should be more realistic. They're simply afraid of expressing emotions, nothing more, nothing less. And that fear makes them very extinguishing with others and, consequently, very boring, very fear-inducing, and very frustrating to be with.

> *Woman*: I think this dress I bought the other day is really pretty!
> *Boyfriend*: How much was it?
>
> *Woman*: I missed you a lot today!
> *Boyfriend*: I was so busy at work, I didn't have time to think. Let me tell you what happened...
>
> *Husband*: I've just been promoted to vice president!
> *Wife*: That's nice. Say, do you want peas or carrots tonight?

Wife: I just got a call from Bex Corporation! They want me to go up and see them about the biggest order our company ever got!
Husband: Well, you'll have to line up a sitter if you're going way out there to see them.

Neutral, non-expressive, extinguishing people kill excitement. They destroy joy. Whose? Anyone with whom they interact frequently. They increase frustration, anger, and fear. Whose? Anyone with whom they interact frequently. We need to consider seriously whether we want people who are so extinguishing around us.

The Effects

Few individuals who like themselves will continue to do so if they are surrounded by people who cannot express feelings openly and spontaneously, especially positive feelings. Indeed, frequent interactions with non-emotionally expressive people can lead us to *fear* liking anything and anyone else. Additionally, interacting with these people will lead to frequent feelings of frustration and anxiety. We each need to decide for ourselves if it's worth it or if it's better to be without this person in our life, even if it means being alone. Indeed, recognizing how common "extinction" is should encourage us to lower our expectations concerning the reactions we want from others, especially over the long term.

Summary

Their behavior toward us	Term	Evaluation	Effect of their behavior
Negative	Punishment	They dislike our behavior	Weakens our behavior
Neutral	Extinction	They don't care or they dislike our behavior	Weakens our behavior
Positive	Reinforcement	They like our behavior	Strengthens our behavior

Having people in our inner circle who frequently criticize or punish others will probably result in our liking fewer things or people in our lives, including ourselves.

Having people in our inner circle who have difficulty being emotionally responsive and who frequently extinguish us will also result in our liking fewer things or people in our lives, including ourselves. They will also increase our frustration, anger, and/or fear.

Everyone is occasionally punishing or extinguishing to others, including us. We must note only the frequent, repetitive behavior of a person.

It is especially important that we step back and note which attitudes, feelings, and behavior *in us* are weakened by the punishment or extinguishing responses of those in our inner circle. This will tell us what their impact will likely be on us over the long term.

Chapter Thirteen

Positive Reinforcement

Now let's look at how our behavior is affected when our friends *like* what we're saying or doing. Trying out our test statement on Cathy, we again say, "You know, Brad and I really get along well. He's such a thoughtful, considerate guy. I'm thinking of dating him." Then we watch Cathy's reaction closely.

Cathy responds emotionally, "Hey, that's great! Brad's adorable! I think you and he are made for each other. And I'm so glad you're finally looking at a thoughtful, considerate guy."

Cathy is happy for us. She has *reinforced* us. This strengthens our behavior of the moment. By responding positively, she increases the strength of our enthusiasm, our liking of Brad, and our joy for life generally. Cathy is a good person with whom to interact frequently if we want someone around who helps us like our decisions and ourself more. If we had a few people like her in our inner circle, we would start becoming more confident, especially in our dealings with others.

What Really Is a Reinforcer?

A reinforcer is usually a response by another person that an individual likes, seeks out, wants to experience. But why does an individual like a particular behavior in others? Because it lessens a fear they have. Since most of our fears center on the behavior of other people, it stands to reason that most things that are reinforcing to us will come from the behavior of other people.

Emotional Reactions as Reinforcers

But what exactly was positive about Cathy's response? As we've said, one of the strongest rewards (reinforcers) in life to most people is experiencing a positive emotional reaction from another person. And that is why Cathy has so much influence on us—her positive emotional reaction. (The physical joys of sex are sometimes not nearly as meaningful as eliciting a positive emotional reaction from one's partner.)

Why is a positive emotional reaction, especially from someone who is important in our lives, so reinforcing to us? Because it momentarily *alleviates so many of our fears*. A positive emotional reaction from someone can momentarily lessen our fear of being disliked, criticized, of feeling someone might be disappointed in us, of being rejected, of feeling alone. No wonder positive emotional reactions are such strong, almost universal positive reinforcers.

We often fear, for example, being insignificant to people in our inner circle, people we truly care about and who we want to truly care about us. An emotional reaction from them tells us we are important to them. A bland reaction (extinction) from someone important to us is frustrating because it tells us we are, or at least might be, insignificant to them.

We also desire a positive reaction from people in our "inner circle" because many of us don't like unhappiness in people we like. And a positive emotional response by them tells us they are happy and we don't have to worry about them. A constant neutral reaction from people important to us, as we have seen, leaves us in limbo, always wondering and worrying, always frustrated in our attempts to bring about some sign of joy and recognition from them.

I Love It When You Yell at Me?

An emotional reaction from others is so important that some people will strive for even a negative reaction from someone significant. This is especially true when the significant other can't express positive feelings.

Some couples seem to be always fighting, screaming and shouting at each other. But they stay together! Why? Because their fear of being unimportant, of being insignificant, of lacking some control or influence over the other person is lessened by their ability to bring out their partner's intense emotional reactions, negative though they may be.

Any reaction is preferable as long as it's emotional. "I don't care if his/her reactions are negative, they're emotional and I brought them on. I influenced, I controlled him/her. Therefore I must be important to him/her." Do people go that far? Some do. Instead of getting caught in that trap, we might first evaluate our prospective friend or mate, see their inability to express positive feelings—and leave. Is being alone a better life than always looking to this constantly non-expressive or negative person to help us enjoy life? That decision is for each of us to make.

Reinforcers as Assessment Tools

Our primary responsibility is to evaluate others and their impact on us. We have seen that people reinforce in others those things that lessen their fear. Consequently, when someone reinforces you, determining why they are reinforcing you will often tell you what they fear. (Again, the reader is reminded to evaluate others *only* in terms of their frequent, repetitive behavior.)

He: You look absolutely gorgeous!
She: Thanks. Say, are Jane and Bill going to dinner with us tomorrow?
Well, she sure doesn't seem too concerned about how she looks to others. She **extinguished** his admiration of her looks.

He: You look absolutely gorgeous.
She: I really find remarks like that quite meaningless. Have you ever thought of focusing on things of substance?

This woman couldn't seem to care less about how she looks to others, since she so dramatically **punished** his admiration of her physical appearance.

He: You look absolutely gorgeous.

She: Oh, my dear, that's so nice of you to say. You're really such a peach.

She fears being unattractive to others (not a difficult analysis, especially since the fear is so common). But how do we know? She emotionally **reinforced** his admiration of her looks; this means he temporarily lessened a fear, in this case a fear over her physical appearance.

She: You're really very important to me.

He: Good. Hey, by the way, are you still available for golf Thursday?

He doesn't seem fearful of being insignificant to her. He **extinguished** her acknowledgment of his importance to her.

She: You're really very important to me.

He: Really? Actually I was just telling some friends of mine about you the other day and how important you are to me. I think about you a lot.

He fears being insignificant to her. He **reinforced** her feelings of his importance to her.

He: I could never leave you.

She: Don't you think that's a little too dramatic?"

Well, she's certainly not afraid of rejection by this fellow. She just **punished** his need for her. (She might feel that he's become too dependent and/or smothering.)

He: I could never leave you.

She: I could never leave you either. We really get along so well together, don't we?

She fears rejection by this guy so she's **reinforcing** his "commitment."

Evaluating our friends periodically is more important than basking in the glory of their compliments, praise, or affection, even if these things do lessen our short-term fears. By evaluating others and their impact on us, we increase the likelihood that we'll take appropriate action for the long term. Then we'll have real hope of reaching a truer state of calmness, contentedness, and increased confidence.

What Is the Best Way to React?

People are often driven by fear. How can we best respond to them in relation to what their behavior might do to us without having to analyze everything first? By always being **cheerful, positive, and enthusiastic** when we're interacting with people. Why? Because these reactions reinforce those who like seeing people happy. Thus, they are reinforcing to those people who want the best for others. And those are the very types of people we want around us.

Cheerful, positive enthusiasm strengthens the tendency of constructive people to say good, positive things to others (us). That helps build our confidence, which is our goal!

If someone compliments you, for example, and you react with good cheer, you'll have strengthened their tendency to compliment you. (Why would they compliment you if they didn't find your happiness reinforcing?) If, on the other hand, someone compliments you and your reaction is one of embarrassment and you mumble some unintelligible response (extinction), good people will compliment you less often. Even worse is the tendency of many of us to deny or argue the compliment (punishment).

Constructive Them: Say, that's really a beautiful blouse.
Cheerful Us: Oh, thank you for saying so! How nice of you to say so!

Thus, if we are positive and cheerful, people who are *good for us*, people who build our confidence, will like us and want to be with us more. That's what we want, people who help us like ourselves, wanting to be with us!

Good Punishes Evil

These same responses of good cheer and enthusiasm by us are *negative* to people who don't like us, want to tear us down, and want us to dislike everything and everyone, including (and especially) ourselves! Enthusiasm is *punishing* to destructive people. Because we're so punishing to them by being of good cheer despite their hurtful behavior, they'll want to avoid us. Perfect!

Destructive Them: Say, that blouse is really old-fashioned. Did you get it at a Salvation Army sale?
Cheerful Us: Yes, and that's why I love it so much!

What is the reinforcer to someone criticizing us? Seeing us upset, hurt, embarrassed. So our good cheer is negative to them. By being cheerful, we punish them, leading them to dislike us. Good! We would do well to avoid people who decrease our self-confidence with as much motivation as we seek out those who increase it.

We don't want people around us who fear our happiness, fear our confidence, our accomplishments, or other people liking us. We want people in our inner circle who want us to be confident, competent, and happy. And if we interact with such people frequently enough, we will be. The way we attract such people to our inner circle is to be as **cheerful, positive, and enthusiastic** as possible. And that's the same way we get destructive people to dislike and stay away from us.

The Temporary Influence of Reinforcers on Fear

While a positive reinforcer is any behavior by someone that lessens our fear, this alleviation of our fear will be only short-lived. People can't go on expressing their positive emotions or compliments or admiration for us every waking moment. As soon as they stop, our old fear will start to return and drive us.

So reinforcing someone will be of little value over the long term with respect to *permanently* lessening their fear-driven behavior. If we frequently reassure a person who feels inadequate, they'll like us. But we will then be getting the "love" of a person whose fear (feelings of inadequacy) will continue to affect us adversely over the long term. It will keep reappearing. And we may not want to be influenced by that particular fear of theirs because we already have enough of our own.

Some examples:
I fear being *insignificant* to my boyfriend. At lunch one day, he tells me that I not only look great but he is awed by my intelligence. He is very reinforcing! I feel confident, good about myself, him, and life. Then he goes back to eating his salad and talking about the problems of his new computer. My fear of being insignificant starts returning and driving my thoughts, feelings, and behavior with him. The positive reinforcer only alleviated my fear as long as it was "on."

I fear being seen as a "wimp" (physically inadequate) by my girlfriend. We have dinner at a nice restaurant but, subconsciously, to show my "toughness" I send my dinner back, complaining that it's too rare (it's not, but my exaggerated behavior is fear-driven). My girlfriend tells me how safe she feels with someone as strong and forceful as me. She is very reinforcing!

Really? I respond, How so? (hoping she'll elaborate). She says she admires my ability to confront people. I adore this woman. Then she turns back to her dinner and starts to talk about her parents' recent separation.

My fear of being seen as "wimpy" returns and leads me to (inappropriately) remark that "only weak people separate." I'm again engaged in inappropriate behavior, wanting her to continue telling me how "strong" I am. The positive reinforcer only alleviated my fear as long as it was "on."

Let's summarize: * Reinforcers generally are behaviors by others that lessen a person's fear. * Reinforcers strengthen the behavior they follow. * Reinforcing someone associates you with the reinforcer and gets them to like you more. * Reinforcers only lessen fears temporarily. * As soon as the reinforcing behavior stops, the fears start returning.

The Frustration and Anger Born of Fear

Few things are more pervasive, important motivators in our lives than our daily goal of alleviating our fear, at least temporarily so that we can get some relief. And few things are more pervasively *frustrating* than our inability to alleviate our fear. This is particularly true when we subconsciously hope or expect the presence of our significant other to do just that, alleviate our fear. That's generally why we "want" someone as a significant other; we subconsciously feel they'll lessen our fear.

We seek as friends those who **share** our fears. We seek as lovers those whom we expect to **lessen** our fears.

When we want to achieve a goal and cannot, our expectations are not realized and we're frustrated. Frustration always leads to anger. As a consequence, when we can't reach our goal of lessening our fear, we become frustrated and angry.

This is one major reason that "significant other" relationships so often bring about strong feelings, including anger that can be inappropriately intense (domestic conflict calls to the police are usually considered among the most dangerous). Why is one's anger so often out of proportion to any behavior their significant other may have engaged in? Because we have such high expectations of the ability of our significant other to lessen our fear, expectations that can rarely be met by anyone.

Suppose I fear being alone. And suppose my *new* significant other, in her enthusiasm over our relationship, calls me every morning at work (which is probably why I like her). Her calls are reinforcing. My fear of being alone is temporarily alleviated. Now suppose my significant other doesn't call me one morning (she had to attend an unplanned, hastily called meeting at work). I become angry. At whom? At her!

Later, at a restaurant, I ridicule her for always ordering the same thing. She and our friends find my anger inappropriate. The anger and ridicule is far out of proportion to her food choice. That's because my fear of being alone is so intense and my expectations of her ability to alleviate it suddenly were not met.

In sum, because of her constant calls, I "fell in love" with her because she practically eliminated my fear of being alone. But she didn't call me today. My expectations are not met. I'm frustrated and I'm angry. My fear is still alive!

What Is Our Relationship?

Personal relationships often bring out fears, hence expectations that we may not have seen in a person when they were "merely" our friend.

Ted fears being insignificant to women who are significant to him. Not having dated anyone in three years has left this fear dormant. Unexpectedly, Ted meets Ann, an attractive woman who seems interesting. Because their discussions are long, deep, and personal, their friendship grows. They develop a close, intimate rapport and soon fall in love.

Their attendance at parties is marked by Ann's close attention to Ted; Ann is telling Ted who is truly significant to her. But one night they go to a party and Ann meets an old friend she hasn't seen in years. They talk on and on, or so it seems to Ted. Ann isn't giving Ted the attention he needs and is accustomed to receiving from her. His fear of being insignificant is not being lessened, hence he starts getting frustrated, then angry.

Later he criticizes the dress Ann wore that night as being too revealing. She's surprised at Ted's behavior; he's never criticized her before. Ted then criticizes her surprised reaction to his "new" behavior, suggesting that perhaps Ann hasn't taken the time to really get to know him. Ann's never seen him like this. Why? Because she continually alleviated his fear, she never knew that the fear existed.

As a friend, Ann did not understand that Ted's fears and expectations were not the same as those a "love" relationship would elicit from him. She doesn't see that it's "her inability" to lessen his fear that caused his frustration and anger.

In sum, friendships do not necessarily lead to good intimate relationships. Personal relationships can bring out fears and unrealistic expectations that just don't exist in friendships. The "perfect" friend can make a terrible lover. And the "perfect" lover can make a terrible spouse.

The Dark Side of Positive Reinforcement

In our desire to be liked, we sometimes use positive reinforcers at the wrong time. **Too often we reinforce and strengthen behaviors that are fear-driven, behaviors that are already excessive and inappropriate.**

Jack is married to a much younger woman. His fear of her leaving him (rejection) is quite strong. As a result, he fears her feeling independent. Jack's fear of losing her to a younger man has led him to be quite controlling and excessively critical. He doesn't want his wife to be independent, but dependent...on him. He doesn't want his wife to trust herself; he wants her to need him. In sum, Jack has a most destructive fear (to his wife), a fear of his wife's liking herself and being confident with her own abilities. (This is not uncommon for many lovers and spouses, no matter what the age difference.)

And Jack's fear leads to extremes of behavior. He tells his wife what to wear, what to say, what golf club to use, and what groceries to buy, and too often criticizes her when she doesn't do what he says. His wife truly loves many things about Jack, but is ready to leave him because of his controlling, critical behavior (Jack's fear is edging him close to the rejection he fears).

Jack's wife sought counsel from a psychiatrist friend. She was advised to lessen Jack's fear of rejection by seeking out his advice and expressing appreciation for it, initiating affection, showing her need for and dependence on him; in other words, she was advised to reinforce him. And these things would indeed reinforce him by *temporarily* alleviating his fear of rejection.

And so, because of her love for him, she did these things. And because she did, he loves her more. That's good. But because he loves her more, he is more fearful than ever of losing her, of her rejection. That's bad. And her "reinforcement" was focused on the very behavior (controlling criticalness) that's already excessive. That's worse. By expressing appreciation for his advice at the wrong time (when he was controlling), she strengthened his controlling behavior. Because she reinforced him by asking for his advice when he criticized her ("What should I do?"), he became critical more often.

Reinforcers do strengthen the behavior they follow. Too often, however, the behavior they follow is fear-driven, already inappropriate. **This is the very behavior we don't want to strengthen.**

Summary

1. People reinforce in others the attitudes, feelings, and behavior they like, i.e., the behavior that alleviates their own fears and makes them feel most comfortable.

2. Reinforcers strengthen the behavior they immediately follow.

3. Watching what behavior our friends reinforce in us (frequently, repetitively) will often tell us who they are and what influence they will have on our feelings and attitudes, our perceptions of them, other people, ourselves, and life over the long term.

4. The emotional reactions of people are some of the strongest positive reinforcers we can experience. Similarly, our emotional reactions, such as our good cheer, strengthen our impact on people.

5. A reinforcer is any behavior by someone that alleviates another person's fear. To know what is reinforcing to someone requires that we know that person's fears.

6. The effects of reinforcers on *fear-driven behavior* are short-lived, transient, and temporary; they are effective in diminishing the fear only as long as the reinforcer is present.

7. Reinforcers are too often used to strengthen fear-driven behavior that is already exaggerated and inappropriate.

8. When someone reinforces us, they're often indicating what their fears are.

9. Different types of relationships with the same person often elicit different fears and expectations, thus different frustrations and angers. Too often, what we want in a friend is what we think we want in a lover. Too often, what we want in a lover is what we think we want in a spouse. Personal relationships often start because our new "friend" frequently reinforces us, thus temporarily diminishing our fears. This raises our expectations of the person and the relationship to unrealistic heights but does nothing to permanently diminish our fears.

Chapter Fourteen

Pairings or Associations

If you smoke this cigarette, people will see you as a rugged individual-ist. If you drink this beer, "fun" people will flock to your side. If you use this mouthwash, that good-looking guy will really enjoy kissing you. These are pairings, or associations, used in advertising. They pair the use of a product with something positive (being seen as rugged, fun people flocking to your side, being kissed by a good-looking guy). This principle of pairings or associations, so important in understanding human behavior, has been virtually ignored by everyone.

Insights from Evaluating the Pairings of People

As we've seen, people talk for one reason: to influence the person(s) with whom they're interacting at the moment. In order to better under-stand someone, we should ask ourselves two questions about them (don't try to do this a lot; it's too difficult):

1. What does this person use most often to influence people, positive (reinforcing) or negative behavior? This will tell us if the person gener-ally likes life and the people in it, or is threatened by life and the people in it. If they tend to use positive associations, interacting with them will lead us to like more things and more people more often. If they are crit-ical and use negative pairings when dealing with others, we will be influenced to dislike and fear things and people more often.

Most people use both positive and negative associations. We want a balance, tipping toward the positive, but always balanced and imbedded in reality. If someone uses *only positives,* they and what they say will eventually mean little to us. We'll quickly see that their fear of being disliked is driving them, and we'll have difficulty taking their opinions seriously. At the other extreme, if someone uses *only negatives,* they will have a pervasively destructive influence on us.

In our lives, we want people with a wide range of behaviors at their disposal, a wide response repertoire, people who are capable of using both positives and negatives—each when appropriate. Who judges what is appropriate for us? We do.

Some people are incapable of using either positives or negatives. These are the quiet, non-expressive people we've already discussed— the people who feel comfortable only with "facts." These are the people who are so often extinguishing, hence frustrating to be with, especially with those with whom they interact at an intimate level.

2. The second question we might *occasionally* ask is: What is the person pairing (or associating) with the positive or negative they are using? Whatever it is, that is what is truly positive or negative to them, and what they want to be positive or negative to us.

An advertisement, for example, might show a woman using a specific detergent, then receiving the emotional appreciation of her family for having made their clothes so "clean and fresh." The ad, of course, is intended to make using this product reinforcing to the consumer by associating the detergent with what is positive to the consumer—the emotional appreciation of her family.

Let's try our two questions on the ad: First, what is being used, a positive or a negative image ? A positive. That is, it's the emotional appreciation of her family that is supposed to be positive to the listener, the consumer. Second, what is being associated with that positive image by the speaker (advertiser)? Using that particular detergent. Then someone *using that detergent* is what is really positive to the speaker, the advertiser.

Another ad shows a woman with a flat tire, alone on a dark road at night. Positive or negative? Negative. What is being paired with the negative? Someone *not* having bought a specific brand of tires. What's negative to the consumer (listener)? Being alone on a dark road. What's negative to the advertiser (speaker)? That is, what are they associating with the negative in the ad? The listener not buying their tires.

Personal Pairings

Pairings are a pervasive force in our personal lives. They have an enormous impact on us. Suppose Sally tells us, "Lee is telling your boyfriend that you're really a selfish person and he'd be better off without you." Our first reaction might be anger toward Lee, then maybe a spirited defense of our lack of selfishness, including many examples.

We'd be far better off evaluating the *speaker*, in this case, Sally. This is more effective than attacking someone not present (Lee), or trying to justify who we are to someone who is present. Our two questions: What did Sally say to us, something positive or something negative? Something negative. What did Sally associate or pair with the negative? Lee. What's negative to Sally? Lee. (Is Lee really telling our boyfriend we're selfish? We have no idea. And we may well want to check it out. But not now. We're dealing with Sally now, and she's the only one we can evaluate and influence.)

Because Sally paired Lee with a negative, we know that she doesn't like him. Who were the words spoken to? Us. Then who was Sally trying to influence? Us. What was she trying to influence us to do? To dislike Lee. How do we know that? Because she paired Lee with negatives *to us!*

(We must always remember, however, to evaluate people in terms of their frequent, repetitive behavior [three of four pairings]. All of us use negative pairings occasionally.)

Where Should We Focus?

We can evaluate only the people with whom we're interacting at the moment. But the people we're interacting with at the moment *often* speak to us about other people who are not present. If they do it excessively (especially with negatives), we must try to minimize their influence on our feelings toward the people they speak about. How? By analyzing the speaker. Besides, it's only the speaker's behavior that is giving us our data for interpretation; when that behavior is excessive and inappropriate, we know we're dealing with a fear. And people's fears are what we are interested in at the moment, because that's what will have the most influence on our attitudes and feelings. Similarly, the only person we can *influence* is the person we're talking to at the moment. Speaking of others is often done under the implied justification that it will somehow help the person who is not there, as though my telling Mary that Jill is too critical will somehow change Jill. Obviously, it won't. And that's not why I say these things. I just want Mary to dislike Jill, pure and simple. And if I'm effective in pairing Jill with things that are negative to Mary, it will change Mary's view of Jill for the worse.

Now Who's Talking About Me?

Let's try a few more examples using our two questions for purposes of analysis. Our friend says, "Larry really respects you."

1. What is this person using, a positive or a negative? A positive. "Respects you" is a strong positive.

2. What is our friend associating with "respects us"? Larry. Conclusion: Our friend likes Larry and wants us to like him also. Do we know anything more about Larry? No. Do we know Larry actually respects us? No, especially if the speaker fears confrontations and is excessively positive in order to please us. If we assume that Larry does

respect us, we could be in for a rude awakening. We must stay with what we know when we're evaluating others: the behavior of the speaker.

A friend says, "Sam is a back-stabber. He criticizes everyone, but never to their face."

1. Is this person using a positive or a negative? A negative. "Back-stabber" is a negative to most people.

2. Who or what is this friend associating "back-stabber" with? Sam. Conclusion: Our friend dislikes Sam and wants us to dislike him also (after all, our friend is talking to us, so he must be trying to influence us). But do we know anything more about Sam? Not really. Our friend's behavior is the only data we have for analysis at the moment.

At a party, a new acquaintance says, "Marriage was one of the best things that ever happened to my parents." Marriage seems quite positive to this person because they're pairing it with a reinforcer.

"I think most people want to get married because they're emotionally or financially insecure." This person paired marriage with a negative. (Several pairings like this can mean there's little marital possibility with this person.)

Opposites Are Not Always Opposite

It's important to focus on evaluating the actual statements of an individual; inferring anything beyond what they are saying can lead to costly mistakes.

"The guys and I always have a great time on these trips."

"The guys" are positive to the person saying this. Does it tell us how he feels about women? No. Don't extrapolate. Don't infer. Don't think in terms of opposites—a love of cold doesn't mean a hatred of hot; liking trips with men doesn't mean a dislike of women. Some men love both and some dislike both.

"I think women today are just plain hostile. They wanted to compete with men, and now they're realizing they don't do too well. Women are just not effective in business."

In this example, "women" have just been associated with negatives. Repeated pairings are what count, and there are three in this example. Thus, we can be fairly certain this speaker does not like women.

But does this person's negative comment about women indicate how he feels about men? No. Later, he could say things like, "Most men are wimps." Three or four comments like this, and we can conclude he dislikes people generally.

Or, this person says, "I really think men are much more capable than women in the vast majority of jobs." From this statement, and a few others like it, we can see that he dislikes women and is more comfortable with men.

God Is in the Details

You're dating a man who asks you to dinner and suggests that you pick the restaurant. When you do so, he says one of two things:

"They have lousy food and worse service." Or he says, "Why would you pick a lousy restaurant like that?" Which comment indicates that this person doesn't like your choice of restaurants and which indicates that he doesn't like you? The *common* element is that both statements use negatives (so this person may not be good to interact with in either case). The *difference* is that the first statement pairs or associates the **restaurant** with the negative—so pick another restaurant. The second pairs or associates **"you"** with the negative, indicating that he may be having some difficulty with you. (A "you," negative pairing is one of the most destructive we'll ever experience; we'll discuss it in more detail shortly).

You're dating a widower. In the course of an intimate dinner, he mentions his lost wife Mary, saying, with a loving glow in his eyes, "You would have liked Mary." Or, he says (with the same loving glow), "Mary would have liked you." Which comment indicates his love for you and which tells you that you may be hearing about his deceased wife for a long time?

The *commonality* is that both are positive, reinforcing comments. Thus, we know this loving person is capable of using positives to influence others. (Excellent! He's probably a good person). The *difference* is that, in the first comment, he associates "you" with the positive. This is a good sign. He likes you! In the second comment, he associates "Mary" with the positive; he stills loves her and is telling you that you're probably going to hear a lot about her in the future. He must miss her and will probably speak of her often during any relationship.

The Ultimate Test

There is little doubt that how we feel about ourselves can have an enormous impact on us and how much we enjoy life. After all, the one thing we can never escape is ourself. So liking oneself would seem to be a very natural thing. Yet, many of us seem to have difficulty doing so.

In looking at why many of us dislike ourselves, two things might be considered. First, the behavior of people in our inner circle has a great influence on how we view ourselves. Second, "anything" associated periodically with negatives by those in our inner circle will start becoming negative to us.

We also saw that a person's "you" pairings, when they're talking to us, will often tell us how they truly feel about us at that time. And it is this "you" pairing that probably has more influence on how we see ourselves than almost any other experience. In sum, one word that should *always* capture our intellectual, analytical, and objective attention is the word "you". When a person is talking to us and says "you," we must watch closely to see if they associate the word with a positive or negative.

"I was really surprised that you didn't get that package for me after I had asked you to pick it up. You don't seem to mind asking me to go out of my way for you." The speaker just associated us with a negative. They have told us, *at that moment,* they're angry with us and that they don't like us. (Remember that frequent, repetitive pairings are the key.) But they're also influencing us to *dislike* ourself!

"I was really surprised that you went out of your way to get that package for me. You're one of the most thoughtful, considerate persons I know." The speaker associated "you" with a positive, thus telling us that, at that moment, they like us. (It's not a bad idea to reinforce the speaker now if you want him to like you.) But he is also influencing us to *like ourself* more.

Conclusion: Positive "you" pairings directed at us *increase* our self-esteem, our confidence, and our respect for ourselves. Negative "you" pairings directed at us have the opposite effect.

If we want to destroy someone's confidence, as some parents do with children, we merely have to pair "you" with negatives: "Why do you always act so stupid?" "Can't you ever do anything right?" "You just never listen, do you?" "Why can't you be well behaved like the Smith child?" "You'll never amount to anything." The child (or adult) bombarded with these types of negative pairings will have great difficulty becoming a confident, independent person.

Positive "you" pairings have the opposite effect; they build confidence. "You're a very special person." "You did a beautiful job there; you did a better job than I could have done." "You're really an intelligent person." "Your advice is certainly respected by a lot of people." "You're one of the most competent, decisive people I've ever had the pleasure of working with."

Conclusion: We must learn to respond with emotional appreciation to these positive "you" pairings ("Thank you for saying so! You're very kind!"). If there is one response in others we want to reinforce and strengthen, it's positive "you" pairings directed at us. Difficulty doing so ("Oh, that's not really true.") is as self-destructive as it is prevalent, accounting for much of the lack of confidence in people generally.

We must keep fairly constant tabs on the "you" association, especially with those in our inner circle who start to pair "you" with negatives. Why? Because they can have such a strong impact on us and how we see ourselves. But we must remember that it's frequent, repetitive associations that tell the true story. ("You" associations are not hard to come by; people use them frequently.)

The "you" association is an extremely volatile one, often fluctuating from moment to moment as feelings change, even in long-term relationships. But if feelings change too frequently and too radically ("you" is first associated with strong positives, then with strong negatives, without apparent reason), there is likely a serious problem in the relationship. Our mate is going through too many emotional conflicts over the relationship. If we don't probe and find the cause, we'll pay a hefty price for his/her conflicts in the long run.

How Important Are Pairings or Associations?

Virtually all prejudices, all social conflicts, and all wars are initially dependent on someone (usually someone in government) pairing a group of people with negatives to another group. Many people, millions of people, can and do die because of these pairings.

Few Americans understand the chronic anger in the Mideast or Africa or Bosnia or Northern Ireland. Why? Because few Americans have been subjected to the pairings that associate a particular group of people in those regions with negatives. The Holocaust would have been far more difficult to carry out if "Jews" had not been frequently paired with negatives by the Nazi regime.

Listen to what the Jewish and Arab "leaders" say to their people about each other, what the Serb leaders say to Serbs about the Croats or

Muslims, what the Hutus say to their colleagues about the Tutsis, what the Catholics say about the Protestants (and vice versa) in Northern Ireland. Think of some of the negative "gay" pairings used by some religious groups in this country. Analyzing these pairings could create greater understanding and, one hopes, less tolerance of the hatreds so often seen in so many areas.

In the United States, the "black-white" issue often involves the same kind of intensely negative pairings. Blacks get many of their views and feelings about whites from other blacks, who often pair whites with negatives. Whites get many of their views and feelings about blacks from other whites, who often pair blacks with negatives. (Even giving examples here would be too inflammatory.)

Human conflicts will continue, in one form or another, until these types of negative pairings are stopped, toned down, or understood by the populace. Conflicts would also decrease quickly if the leaders of one group started pairing "the other group" with positives, instead of negatives, to their own group, an unlikely event in many instances.

Summary

1. People use positives and negatives in their interpersonal relationships. We want to be with people who use positives more often than negatives.

2. Who or what a person pairs with a positive concept or statement tells us who or what they like and/or who or what they want us to like.

3. Who or what a person associates with a negative is what they dislike and want us to dislike too.

4. When we're evaluating a person, we should focus on the "who" or the "what" they're pairing with the positives or negatives. And that is often the most important thing we can do (the alternative is to let their influence "wash" over us indiscriminately). By analyzing the speaker, we diminish that person's influence on our feelings, especially toward other

people. We might particularly want to diminish this influence on us when the speaker's pairings are excessively critical and negative.

5. We should be constantly   alert for "you" pairings directed at us, especially by those in our inner circle.

6. Those who pair "you" with a positive are indicating that they like us (at least at that moment). Experiencing "you" reinforcer pairings increases our self-confidence. We should emotionally reinforce and strengthen any speaker who gives us positive "you" pairings. This will increase the frequency of those cherished positive "you" pairings, thus further increasing our confidence.

7. If a person frequently pairs "you" with negatives, they dislike us and want us to dislike ourselves. They will do great damage to our confidence. We should avoid them or, at least extinguish them when they make such pairings. (An "upset" reaction by us, or a response of emotional anger, reinforces those who give us negative "you" pairings, since upsetting us is the goal of anyone who gives us negative "you" pairings).

8. It is only frequent, repetitive pairings that offer a solid criterion by which we should judge a person.

Chapter Fifteen

Who People Are to Us

We would do well to consider what we want in our friends and in a partner. Too often, we focus on what we don't want and/or don't like in others. This results in an overly critical orientation on our part. Knowing what we want in others gives us a target to shoot for, rather than something to shoot at.

Our overall goal is to find people who are able to display a wide range of reactions to various situations encountered by everyone in life. We also want a significant other who has a minimum of excessive behaviors (accepting the fact that everyone has some). In sum, we want someone who is as confident as possible. But there are two special behaviors in people we would do well to focus on.

Liking People

Liking people is one of the most important criteria of confidence in a person. Anyone who does not like people can't be truly confident; people are just too pervasively present in our lives. It would be similar to someone fearing plants and living in the jungle; the fear would be just too constant.

If we like people, we'll express our positive feelings to them in many subtle ways, through behaviors we cannot consciously force ourselves to engage in. What's the effect of that? People will like us! No one can resist liking someone who truly likes (not needs) them.

Those Who Dislike People Will Influence Us

If the people in our inner circle dislike people, they will associate people with negatives to us. "People are so selfish," or "John is telling everyone you're cheap," or "Mary really isn't doing her fair share; you should talk to her." This cannot help influencing us to start disliking people. And the opposite of "like" is not dislike or hate...it's fear.

We'll also be *punished or extinguished* for liking other people by those who don't like people. Worse, we'll be *reinforced* for disliking people, thereby strengthening our wary suspicions of others. And these negative feelings in us will be apparent to those with whom we interact frequently, compromising our constructive relationships. It's not pretty, but it's true. People in our inner circle have just too strong an influence on us.

Love Thyself?

What is the most important thing in a person's life, to like themselves or to like other people? Most would agree that it is to like yourself. But most would be wrong. Please remember that the people we see frequently have a strong influence on us, and on our attitudes and feelings toward others and ourselves. If we learn to dislike people, they will soon learn to dislike us. If people dislike us, we will soon learn to dislike ourselves. (On the other hand, if we dislike ourselves, but like people, they will soon influence us to like ourselves.)

Consequently, as we get to know people, we must especially note whether they associate people with positives or negatives. We must note whether they reinforce or punish our liking of people. We must determine whether they seek out and enjoy interactions with people or are so shy, withdrawn, or angry that they avoid them.

The Attraction of Those Who Dislike People

Unfortunately, many of us are attracted to withdrawn people who fear and avoid others. Why? Because we fear being rejected, abandoned, or compared unfavorably with others. Thus, we feel safe and secure with someone (especially a significant other) who dislikes, condemns, criticizes, and avoids other people; after all, they are unlikely to leave us for another person, for any "competition." After all, they don't like anyone.

So we're comfortable with, and confident of, their "loyalty." This is a mistake. We'll also soon learn from them to dislike and distrust people. Then people will learn to dislike and distrust us. Then they will reject us. So our fear will get us what we fear (being rejected), a phenomenon we've seen over and over again.

And who do those who dislike people usually select as best friends? Those who also dislike people. Why? Because their fears won't be confronted; they will find comfort in each other, since neither is likely to demand that they interact with others. Worse, they will continually reinforce each other for not liking people. They have a common interest, a common bond—their dislike (fear) of people and anyone liking people.

Emotional Expressiveness

The second quality we must have in people in our inner circle is the ability to exude a positive *emotional expressiveness*. As we've seen, a positive emotional reaction from another person is one of the strongest, most pervasive, and sought-after reinforcers to people.

Most of us fear being unimportant to others, especially significant others. How do we know we are important to others? Because they respond emotionally to us. Those who don't react emotionally are the "extinguishers" who are so frustrating to be with.

Feeling that we're insignificant to people means we feel that we have no influence over them. Influencing people is the one desire that is in virtually all of us. Why is influencing others so important? Because we all fear something in the behavior of people. We may each have fears that are a little different from the fears of others, but we all want to influence people, to prevent them from engaging in the particular behavior we fear. And if we have little or no influence over them, they may engage in our feared behavior readily and frequently.

Positively Expressive

An emotional reaction from someone has a strong influence on people, including us. So there is another qualification to expressiveness that must be considered. Those in our inner circle must be able to be emotionally expressive in *positive* areas. In negative areas, an emotional reaction is disastrous!

"That guy is really great! He can return a serve better than anyone I've ever seen," says someone in our inner circle. This speaker is a good person to know. He doesn't have any inhibitions over describing other people enthusiastically. If this behavior is typical (frequent, repetitive) of this person, we'll be more positive and confident toward life and people if we interact with this person a lot.

"That guy's a real loser! He can't tell the difference between his head and a hole in the wall!" is a remark that means trouble for us if it's frequent, repetitive behavior of someone in our inner circle. And if, because of their fear, this behavior is extreme, then this person's influence on us will be quite destructive, inciting us to dislike people more.

While the first person is enthusiastic, the second is hostile, capable of verbal and possibly even physical abuse. How do we know this? The response is too outspoken, too blunt and direct. It not only tells us this person is emotional in negative areas, but that they will openly express it. And their influence will be negative, stirring in us fear and anger. (Don't admire their "forcefulness," especially if you're not forceful. Merely note that their hostile behavior is extreme and inappropriate, hence fear-driven. And their fear of people will infect those who interact a lot with them; that shouldn't be us.)

When a person is emotionally expressive, watch their orientation. Is their expressiveness positive or negative? Either way, their influence on you will be strong. If positive, wonderful! If negative, or there is no emotional expressiveness, reconsidering a relationship with them may be in order.

What's best? A *realistic emotional* expressiveness, sometimes positive and sometimes negative, but above all, balanced. Who is balanced? People who respond realistically to their environment. If the movie is bad, they say so. If the movie is good, they say so. But if, to them, *every* movie is good or *every* movie is bad, than you know their behavior is extreme and fear-driven; you may want to reevaluate the relationship. But who sets the criteria for good or bad? In your life, you do. After all, you're the individual the other person is trying to influence.

What You Use to Influence Others is What You'll Become to Others

There are, as we have seen, three manners in which we can respond to the behavior of other people: positively, neutrally or negatively. Which one we use will determine who we are to people. Why? Because we pair or associate ourselves with the response we use.

Using positives (good emotional reactions) to get what we want from people associates us with those positives. It makes the other person feel comfortable with our attempts to influence him/her because our positives (as do all positives) alleviate their fear.

"Why don't you wear that gray coat? You always look so good in it. When you wear it, everyone tells me how handsome you are." This association gets the person to like both wearing the gray coat and the speaker more. Why? Because whenever you use a positive with someone, you're associating or pairing yourself with it.

Using negatives to influence people makes us negative to those people because we're associating ourselves with those same negatives. "Oh, don't wear that gray coat. You always look so fat in it. That coat makes you look like a stuffed pig." This will indeed lead the person to dislike the gray coat a little more. Unfortunately, because the speaker used a negative, she also associated herself with the negative. Thus, the person dislikes both the gray coat and the speaker a little more.

Being neutral (no emotional reaction, bland) all the time means we don't allow ourselves to care about anyone, hence we don't show an interest in anything. "I really don't care what coat you wear." Unfortunately, as we have seen, this non-emotional reaction leads to frustration and anger in the other person. ("Well, hell then, I just won't wear any coat.")

You are to people what you use to influence them. If you use positives, you'll associate yourself with them and become more desirable to others. If you rely on negatives or non-reactions (extinction) to influence people, you'll become less desirable to others.

This is one major reason it's important to know what you want in a significant other, rather than to focus on what you dislike in them. If you focus on what you want, you're more likely to use positives to get it, associating yourself with positives in the process. If you focus on what you dislike in a significant other, you're likely to use negatives to punish them for their behavior; this associates you with the negatives, probably making for a stormy relationship.

Focus Outside Yourself

What does our potential friend use to influence us? Does he know what he wants and use positives to strengthen it? "I think your laughter lights up the room."

Does he focus on what he dislikes and use negatives to stop whatever it is? "You really shouldn't smile until you get that tooth fixed; you look awful."

Or does he respond neutrally to us and people generally? "That's interesting, but I've really got to get this project done. Can we talk about it some other time?"

Let's summarize some points and their potential dangers:

1. What a person uses to influence others—positives or negatives or neutrals—is what they associate with themselves. And what they associate with themselves is what they will eventually become to us. If they use positives to reinforce us and influence us to get what they want, they are likely to become positive to us. Then we'll want to be with them more.

That's why it's crucial to know what a person wants and likes in us. If they want the wrong thing, we might soon be doing that more often because of their reinforcing influence. If, for example, someone likes our sadness or our anger toward others, they might well reinforce it. Because they used a reinforcer and associated themselves with it, we'll like them and want to be with them more. But we'll also become more depressed or angry because we are being reinforced for being so. This is a dangerous situation and accounts for some of those people who seem so attracted to partners who are bad for them. It's not enough that someone reinforces us; we must make sure that what they want in us, what they reinforce us for being, is good for us.

2. If a person always uses negatives to suppress what they don't like in others, people will always feel criticized and chastised by them. And no one will know what the person does want in others. And some people, we should realize, don't want anything; they just want to criticize. Or worse, they just use negatives to elicit the behavior they really want from others—a hurt, fearful, embarrassed, tearful, or angry reaction. Why do they want that? Because they're fearful of someone's happiness. One would hope that all but the most masochistic individuals will avoid

them. People of this sort truly fear anyone liking themselves and, if we interact with them enough, they'll probably achieve that goal.

3. If a person always responds neutrally, we will never know what they want or what pleases them. But we will know that no matter what it is, we're unable to give it to them. Consumed with our own inadequacies, frustrations, and angers, we'll never realize that they're *afraid* to want or like anything. We'll learn to dislike them, other people, and life itself (even though we hopelessly but continually strive to please them). Worse, we'll learn to dislike ourselves.

Everything Can Be Good

Negative emotional reactions are sometimes appropriate. Neutral emotional reactions are sometimes appropriate. Positive emotional reactions (more often than not) are sometimes appropriate. And all are inappropriate at times. It depends on the frequency, the excessiveness, and the timing. We want people in our inner circle who have a wide response repertoire. We want people who can engage in all three reactions, each at the appropriate time. Who judges the appropriate time? For your life, you do.

Summary

We want at least two special things in those in our inner circle:
1. A love of people and a love of our love of people.
2. An ability to be enthusiastic and emotionally responsive in positive areas.

We determine if others meet these criteria by watching what they reinforce, punish, extinguish, and associate with positives and negatives. It is our liking of people that we want them to reinforce in us.

People are to us what they associate themselves with when trying to influence us, whether it be positives, negatives, or neutrals. So, too, are we to others what we use to influence them. If we know what we want and use positives to get it, we'll be liked and often get want we want.

If we focus on what we don't like and use negatives to stop or prevent others from doing those things, we'll be negative to others. We may, through our use of negatives, successfully prevent people from doing what we don't want them to. But in no way does this mean we'll get them to do what we do want.

Knowing what we want in others is one of the most constructive orientations we can have when interacting with people and building our inner circle of friends. Knowing what those in our inner circle want in us is crucial in building our confidence and happiness.

Chapter Sixteen

Interpreting the Behavior of Others

Whoever asks the questions controls the interaction. Asking a question determines the focus of the dialogue between two or more people. It tells most people where they must turn their attention if they are to behave in a civilized manner. Because asking questions is so important, we must learn to do so correctly—and we will in this and the chapters that follow. But first we must understand the goal of our questions—to evaluate people and their potential influence on us over the long term.

Content Versus Behavioral Interpretations

There are two ways to interpret another person's behavior. One is the "normal" way, the way we have been taught to react all our lives. This involves focusing on what the person is saying. We'll call this, appropriately enough, a **content** interpretation. The other way to interpret behavior is quite different. It involves focusing on what the behavior is telling us about the person, regardless of what they are talking about. Here we're reacting to what they are talking about only insofar as it indicates who they are and how they would influence our attitudes and feelings. This we'll call a **behavioral** interpretation. We should do these only occasionally. Let's look at a clarifying example of a content and a behavioral interpretation.

"I went to Greece last year, and it was beautiful! The islands were peaceful, really inspiring. The water was unbelievably clear, and I loved swimming in it. It was one of the best vacations I ever had!"

Content interpretation: Maybe I should consider Greece for my next vacation.

Here we are *not* thinking of the person doing the talking, just the thing they are talking about (Greece). This is the way we have been taught to think and the way we should think most of the time.

Behavioral interpretation: This person is positive and enthusiastic. How do we know this? They just were.

Here we're looking at what the person is saying only insofar as it tells us something about that person. We don't even care about Greece, nor are we focused on it. The person could just as easily have been talking about widgets, dogs, or stairs. It is the *person* we're focused on—in this case, their positive enthusiasm. (Remember we judge people in terms of their frequent, repetitive behavior; one response tells us little. So they must speak enthusiastically several times—at least three—before we firmly arrive at this conclusion.)

"I went to Athens last year, and it was awful! The air was filthy, the people were surly, and getting around by car was impossible because the people don't have an inkling of how to drive."

Content interpretation: I should be hesitant about going to Athens on my next vacation.

The person has associated Athens with negatives and tried to influence our views about that particular city. And Athens (content) is what we're focused on and reacting to. We're not even thinking about the person. If they had spoken about widgets as negatively as they did about Athens, our views about widgets would be influenced as negatively as they have been about Athens.

Behavioral interpretation: This person is negative and overly critical.

Here we're focusing on the behavior and what it tells us, not about Athens, but about the person. We don't even care about Athens. What we're learning is that this person's behavior could influence us to be negative and critical if we choose to be with them. (Frequent, repetitive behavior is the criterion; one response tells us little. That's why we keep repeating this statement frequently and repetitively.)

Let's try a few more interpretations:

We're at a party with a lot of strangers and a casual male acquaintance says, "These things always make me nervous. I'm uncomfortable meeting new people." Is this person confident or not?

If we do a content interpretation, we must say they are not confident; after all, they just told us they are nervous. A behavioral interpretation tells us just the opposite, however; telling someone they are nervous is a very confident response, especially for a male in this macho age. That is, the person has the confidence to say to someone else, "I'm nervous, I'm afraid."

This person probably has a wide response repertoire. The "macho" male has a narrow response range precisely because he cannot engage in this type of behavior.

* * *

A man slams his hand down on the table angrily, declaring, "I do not get angry!"

Content interpretation: This person is well controlled and does not get angry. How do we know? He just said so and, if we follow and believe in content interpretations, we must say so too!

Behavioral interpretation: This person is too violently emotional. He gets angry and loses his temper too easily. How do we know? He just did behaviorally, regardless of the content of what he said.

* * *

"I really dislike superficial people. By the way, I have a real dilemma tonight. There are two great shows on TV at exactly the same time. Can you believe that? Now I don't know which one I should watch and which one I should tape. I really can't believe they'd do that."

> *Content interpretation:* This person dislikes superficial people and thus must have a deep, profound personality.

> *Behavioral interpretation:* The content interpretation is wrong. This person is quite superficial despite (because of?) their remark implying the contrary.

* * *

Making the Switch

The switch from content to behavioral interpretation can be difficult to make. We will always have some trouble doing it. That's because we must necessarily focus on content most of the time. When a store clerk tells us how much our total bill comes to and what our correct change is, we can't sit back and try to determine whether or not he is enthusiastic and positive. This is not a time for behavioral analysis. Similarly, when a boss tells us how she wants the job done, we'd do well to listen to content.

But when we're considering a personal relationship with someone with whom we are, or might be, interacting frequently, and/or when that someone is a part of our inner circle, it is essential that we swing our focus to a behavioral orientation periodically. When we develop personal relationships, we are subjecting ourselves to the influence of the other person's behavior on us, especially their fear. How that person feels about a particular movie may be important to us for the moment. But over the long term, the frequent, repetitive attitudes and feelings of that person will have an enormous influence on who we are and become.

The Fears of the Person

What we really want to determine are the fears of the person.

We know that fear leads to specific excessive behavior patterns. And we know that all excessive behaviors are driven by fear. So we are especially watchful for excessive behaviors in an individual.

Frequent, repetitive behaviors tells us who the person is. Excessive, inappropriate behaviors tell us what the person's fears are. We want to know both, but especially the latter.

If the positive person is *always* positive, always "bubbly and cheerful," then they are *excessively* positive, hence their behavior is inappropriate. Then we know we are dealing with a fear. What fear? Well, what do they have difficulty doing? Behaving in a critical, negative way. They may well have difficulty assuming an aggressive stance and confronting negative issues.

Why would someone fear being critical and negative? Well, fear always involves the behavior of other people. As we've seen, maybe they avoid expressing negative views because they fear being disliked. Thus, they fear argumentative interactions, confrontations, or just being seen by people as being too negative.

Incidentally, we'll never fully understand how people came to be the way they are, and we really shouldn't care. It's fun to guess the why's or how's of people's lives, but it is always guesswork and of little ultimate value. Indeed, many people are more than happy to explain the abuse they endured that led to their fears, if only to get our sympathy. It's who they are, and what their impact on us will be, that must be our focus.

If the negative person *never* (or rarely) expresses positive comments, we conclude they are *excessively* negative. Thus we know we're dealing with a fear. We hypothesize that they are frightened of being positive. Why are they? Maybe because anyone liking anyone (including them) or liking anything else in life is threatening to them. (Many teenagers and macho men have been punished by their "tough" friends for expressing positive behavior because such behavior is often seen as "naive," "wimpy," and/or "feminine.")

If people can express both positive and negative feelings, they probably have a wide response range and are more likely to be balanced and confident.

In summing up the above examples, the key word is *excessive*. If behaviors are excessive, they are driven by fear. We have seen that the goal of fear-driven behavior is to prevent some behavior in others. In the excessively positive person, it may be a fear of confrontations or of being disliked. In the excessively negative person, it may be a fear of intimacy or of being seen as weak or of even being liked.

What a Person's Friends Tell Us

Some excessively critical, hostile people fear and will attack the enthusiasm of anyone over anything and everything. As a result, the friends of hostile, critical people rarely "like" anyone or anything. They can be quite negative and critical too. Since the friends of an individual often share their fears, they often provide a good source of information about the individual.

Just as macho often surrounds itself with macho, so also does the highly sensitive person frequently collect highly sensitive friends, avoiding more blunt and abrasive individuals. Consequently, assessing the commonality of fears of those in an individual's inner circle can often provide useful insights into the individual.

Learning To Evaluate Others

It's important to realize that we can't focus on both content and behavior at the same time when talking to someone. That's generally too complex a task for the human mind. In most instances, we should focus on content. It helps us relate realistically to people and gets us through life a little easier. When we're thinking of developing relationships, however, we would often do well to focus periodically on behavior and what it tells us about the person rather than what they're talking about.

Evaluate First

We all want to influence certain people in our lives. But evaluating a person before we try to influence them allows us to know what is important to them and what is not. Knowing a person allows us to be aware of what can be confronted and what should be avoided, what is changeable and what is not changeable. Thus, we are much better off assessing a person before we try to influence them and/or allow them to enter our inner circle.

Why is evaluating someone in the initial stages of a possible relationship so important? First, it allows us to determine if we want to continue seeing them. Second, as the relationship progresses, our emotions will become more influential and we will lose much of our objectivity. Then we will be more driven by our desire to influence them than by our more important need to understand them, who they truly are, and how they will affect us.

Asking questions of someone in order to accurately evaluate them should *always* be our first goal, a goal that will be much easier to reach in the initial stage of the relationship when they aren't as important to us.

The Goal of Evaluations

What we are looking for is a person's frequent, repetitive behavior. This is truly who they are. This is who they'll be with us over the long

term. This is the behavior that will affect us, and our attitudes and feelings if we build a relationship with them.

We all have times when we're not "ourselves." So if someone is overly
critical or excessively non-responsive, we'll take note of it. But we'll
continue to "interview" them. And if we consistently get overly critical
views, we'll conclude that this is who this person is…frequently and
repetitively. Two or three instances should be enough. (Even the rule of
"frequent, repetitive" can be ignored, however, if the behavior is
outrageous, e.g., if the person expresses an acceptance of the "inferiority
of women" or the admiration of physical violence.)

What should we know about someone? One thing above all else:
what they fear. And what do most people fear? The actions of others,
potential or real. We have to find out what actions or behaviors the person fears from others—what behavior (criticism, rejection, being
ignored, being controlled, being seen as inadequate) they try to prevent
in others.

Summary

A content interpretation focuses on the thing, idea or person that the
person is talking about at the moment.

A behavioral interpretation focuses on the frequent, repetitive
patterns or commonalities in a person's behavior. This tells us who the
person is and what impact they'll have on us. It is their behavior,
especially their fears, that will have the greatest impact on us over the
long term. Indeed, the success or failure of most long-term
relationships will be determined by the fears of the individuals involved
and how those fears conflict with each other.

Generally, we cannot focus on both content and behavior at the
same time. When we have a relationship with someone or are thinking of building one, we should *periodically* swing our focus to behavioral interpretations.

Chapter Seventeen

Five Principles of Drawing Out Open, Spontaneous Behavior

In order to assess someone, we need a sample of their behavior. The best way to get this sample is to ask some questions. But our sample can't be just any behavior; it must be typical of the individual. This requires that we follow some guidelines in asking questions.

These guidelines should also allow us to build rapport with a person, to lead them to feel we care about them. Thus, if we're adept at asking questions, people will like us and want to be with us. Whether or not we want to be with them should be answered by our sample of their typical behavior.

When Is Evaluation Appropriate?

The goal of asking questions is to be enabled to make accurate and insightful interpretations. But those insights will depend entirely on an ability to draw out another person's spontaneous and open behavior effectively. The inability to accurately understand/interpret behavior is almost always a result of an inability to do a good job of bringing out spontaneous behavior from the other person.

The types of questions we'll discuss are almost always appropriate when interacting with people, e.g., at a party, at work, with strangers, with bosses and with subordinates, with spouses and children, and especially—and most important of all—with significant others. Having the ability and skill to focus on others and ask them meaningful questions periodically can put the most uncomfortable of them (and us) at ease. It will allow the most withdrawn, shy person to meet strangers and control interactions.

We need to put a temporary hold on our need to discuss ourselves, our views and opinions and, instead, focus completely on the other person. Most important, we need a calm, evaluative orientation. This mind-set has no room for our normally frequent desire to try to interject our views and try to influence the thinking of the other person (especially about us). It's just not time yet. We must know the person first if we hope to try to influence them effectively (or even if we want to put forth the effort to influence them at all).

The Five Principles of Asking Questions

There are five principles we'll rely on to bring out a sample of someone's typical behavior, understand them and their fears, tell them we care about them and, as a result, get them to care about us. These principles will first be summarized, then will be discussed in depth.

1. Be *nonjudgmental*. Using this stance, we encourage people to be spontaneous, to be who they truly are. Being nonjudgmental alleviates their fear of being criticized.

2. Ask *broad, general questions*. In doing so, we allow people to focus on what's important, interesting, and reinforcing to them. This is what they feel "safe" with.

3. *Probe their responses*. Asking for further information shows people that we are interested in them (then they'll probably be interested in us). Our probing alleviates their fears of how they are being seen by us, their fear of being seen as boring, insignificant, or unimportant.

4. Use *a soft, gentle, inflected tone of voice*. This encourages people to feel comfortable and spontaneous, rather than threatened by us. A gentle, inflected tone shows respect and alleviates their fear of being challenged, dominated, insulted, or involved in some kind of competition with us.

5. *Let the other person lead the way. Whenever possible, base questions on some part of their last response.* In doing so, we tell people that we really are listening to them and want to discuss things they want to discuss. Because we follow their lead, we alleviate their fear of being controlled by us.

Being Nonjudgmental

A nonjudgmental attitude is what separates the successful approach to evaluations from the unsuccessful. No matter what we feel, we say nothing about our views. Why? Because we're not trying to influence the person; we're trying to evaluate them.

When we meet someone new at a party or on a blind date, we will minimize the expression of our preferences, our likes or dislikes. We want to hear from the other person. We respond with respect and concern to anything they say and any view they hold. If we think a movie stinks and our "partner" thinks it deserves an "Oscar," we listen respectfully to their reasoning and analysis. We do not express negative views or argue with them or try to impress them with our more "brilliant" analyses.

As a result, the person feels "safe" and able to be spontaneous. Why? Because they see that we're interested in their opinions; we're not trying to get them interested in ours. Their spontaneity is what we want. And because we're *nonjudgmental,* their spontaneity is what we'll get. Most important, we accept what they say, without judgment. Only with interest.

If we're judgmental, on the other hand, we'll make the person uneasy and concerned over our reactions to their opinions. Then we'll start to bring forth behavior that may not truly represent them—behavior that reflects their concern about our reactions.

If we tell them they're being too negative and overly critical, they may become much less so. But too negative and overly critical may exactly describe them. By punishing and suppressing such feelings with our judgmental disapproval, we may be led to "fall in love" with them, only to make the painful discovery later that they're really negative and critical. Trying to influence people prevents us from knowing who they truly are, or who they will be, or what impact they will have on us over the long term. We'll only know who they want us to think they are.

Tripping Over Our Feelings. Being nonjudgmental when interacting with other people is emotionally difficult because we have to ignore our views and opinions and focus on theirs.

> *Husband* (in a moment of unusual curiosity): How am I as a husband?
> *Wife:* You're all right.
> *Husband* (angrily): Now what in hell is that supposed to mean?

This husband doesn't want to know his wife's true views. He wants to influence her, to control her, to "make" her appreciate him through punishment and coercion.

> *Husband:* How am I as a husband?
> *Wife:* You're all right.
> *Husband* (gently): How so?

Now we're getting somewhere. He didn't punish her by responding in a negative, angry way. He wasn't judgmental. Now he'll probably find out how his wife truly feels. He may not like it, but he'll start to learn what he can and cannot expect from her, where he can and cannot go with her, what he can and cannot do with her. He'll also start building rapport with her by communicating his interest in how she truly feels rather than his insistence that she conform to his wishes about how she should feel.

> *Sandy:* What do you think of Brad?
> *Mary:* I don't like him.
> *Sandy:* You really don't like anyone, do you?

Sandy is being judgmental. She is not really concerned about who Mary truly is, how Mary thinks about Brad, and how Mary will affect her. Sandy's concern is in trying to change Mary's views of Brad.

> *Sandy:* What do you think of Brad?
> *Mary:* I don't like him.
> *Sandy* (gently): Because?

Excellent! Sandy will now start to learn who Mary is, what Mary feels about people and, most important, what impact Mary may have on Sandy over the long term.

Evaluating Versus Influencing Someone. As previously mentioned, the only person we can both understand and influence is the person with whom we're interacting at the moment. Let's be clear about our goals when interacting with someone. Do we want to understand them or influence them? Since it's difficult to effectively influence someone without understanding them, we must evaluate first, then influence.

"Don't ever go into a relationship with the idea of trying to change someone." All reasonable people tell us this. But if we're going to build a relationship with someone, we're going to have to adjust to them and they to us. That means change…by both parties. We want to make those changes and adjustments as smooth and painless as possible. This means making sure that our expectations reflect reality.

Now is the time to learn who the person is, what influence they'll have on us, what we'll attempt to change in them, how we can best do it, what about them is unchangeable and whether we should even try to change them at all. Having the patience and taking the time to know who a person truly is during our initial interactions with them can save us from wasting months or even years of our lives.

Asking Broad, General Questions

Since asking questions gives us so much control, we tend to ask too many questions in areas that reflect our own interests. Bringing forth a person's typical behavior requires that we give *them* control in picking the topic. We're only looking for a sample of their behavior. Our questions, consequently, should allow the person as much leeway as possible in responding. So we'll throw out **broad, general questions** that are somewhat ambiguous and allow the other person to respond to in any way they wish. Let's look at some good and bad examples:

Bad: Where do you live?
Good: How is the neighborhood where you live?

Bad: How long have you known Bill?
Good: What's Bill like?

Bad: When did you leave St. Louis?
Good: How was St. Louis?

Bad: Who is your boss?
Good: What kind of a person is your boss?

Bad: How long have you worked for your company?
Good: What's the atmosphere like there?

Bad: When's the last time you saw a good movie?
Good: What do you look for in movies?

Bad: How long have you been a pilot?
Good: How do you like flying?

Bad: When did you get a divorce?
Good: What kind of a person is your ex-wife?

Bad: When will you move to New York?
Good: How do you feel about moving to New York?

Give the other person leeway. Let them be spontaneous and go where they wish to go. Let them be who they are, because that's precisely what we want to know. It's not the right time to force them to focus on what we're interested in so we don't get bored. It's not the right time to try to impress them. It's not the right time to try to make them who we think they should be or who we wish they were.

Response to Narrow Versus General Questions. The typical response to factual questions (such as those above labeled "bad") will frequently offer us little to interpret. Broad, general questions often open the gates of spontaneous, diverse behaviors that offer meaningful interpretations and important knowledge for us. Consider the following typical responses to narrow versus general questions:

"I've been with my company three years" tells us little. "My company has a lot of problems, such as…" can tell us a great deal.

"I met Bill at a party" doesn't tell us much. "What I like about Bill is his thoughtfulness. He's one of the most considerate…" can tell us a lot.

"I started flying when I came out of the Navy" is of little real consequence. "I love the freedom of flying, of being away from anyone telling me what I should or shouldn't do…" can tell us a great deal.

"I've been divorced three years" is of some, but little value. "My ex-wife is a real bitch and I'd like to strangle her" offers us more insightful conclusions (and more effective remedies, such as, "Say, I think I see someone over there by the punch bowl I haven't seen in years; excuse me").

"I moved here six months ago" can lead everyone (including the speaker) to yawn in boredom. "I like it here because the people seem so friendly and outgoing. I've probably made more friends…" opens up the possibility of relevant interpretations.

A relaxed person is an open, spontaneous person. By throwing out broad questions, we're also putting the person at ease. We're alleviating their fears even though we're subtly controlling the interaction by asking these questions. By asking general questions, however, we're letting the person go anywhere they want. We're not asking them "test" questions by putting them on the spot regarding their opinions, ready to pounce if "they're wrong."

Our broad, general questions tell them there are no right or wrong answers, that anything they say is perfectly acceptable to us. Our nonjudgmental reactions to their responses tells them we respect anything they say and any point of view they hold.

The Safety of Broad, General Questions. Using broad, general questions and allowing the person to discuss whatever they like also tells us two important things: (1) what the person feels most comfortable talking about and (2) what the person is most interested in.

Knowing what the person feels comfortable talking about suggests other areas we can explore, what we can focus on without inhibiting or frightening them. When asked what their company is like, some people will focus on interpersonal relations in the company, while others focus on the bottom line growth of the company. In either case, we will know what area is safe to discuss with them.

Letting the person respond any way they wish to our broad, general questions allows them to "lead" the conversation by providing us with subject matter that's important to them; it tells us what they value. They're almost guaranteed an interesting conversation with us; after all, they're picking the topics. We now know what area we should focus on in our next question. We know what will show them that we're truly listening to them and that we're really interested in what they're saying.

But Do We Really Care? It is true, however, that most people will respond to our general questions in a perfunctory way. "How is it being a realtor?" will often get an answer of "It's OK." And these are often the same perfunctory answers we'll get to good questions like: "How was the movie?" or "What's Bill's personality like?"

Why do these good questions get perfunctory answers? Because most people have learned that the questioner is really not interested in their views at all. Because the person who asked the question usually starts talking about something else after they got a perfunctory answer to their broad, general questions. Consider the following all too probable responses to an individual's typical answers:

>*Good question:* What's Bill's personality like?
>*Them:* I think Bill's a pretty nice guy.
>*Bad response:* Let me tell you about a hellava good guy I met once.
>*Worse response:* You know, my husband is...
>*Terrible response:* I really think all most men care about is...

* * *

>*Good question:* How do you like your apartment?
>*Them:* I like it a lot.
>*Bad response:* You know, I once looked at apartments in that building.
>*Worse response:* I remember an apartment I once had in Sacramento. It...
>*Terrible response:* I used to think renting was the way to go, but after doing a careful analysis, I concluded...

The Best Follow-Up Question: The Probe

We're going to shock this person when they respond to our broad, general question in a perfunctory way. How? By probing! What is a probing question? A probe is a short, quick, inquisitive question that asks our "new friend" *for more.* A probe tells someone we're interested in them and what they're saying because it asks them to elaborate on their last response.

Some probes: **How so? Because? In the sense of?**

The Art of Probing

No behavior will tell you more about a person than the behavior you draw out by probing. Why? Because you're asking them to elaborate on their feelings, attitudes, and concerns. And you're *not* asking them to do so in order to argue with them or belittle them. You're nonjudgmental. You're not trying to influence them or impress them with your astute analyses. So the only reason you could be probing is because you're really interested in what they're saying. And with such a respectful, receptive audience, a person will be more likely to be open and spontaneous, and tell you exactly who they are. Probes bring out the most meaningful behavior for our interpretations.

> *Us:* How is Bill as a person?
> *Them:* Good.
> *Us:* How so?

They will now feel two things: (1) Oh, you really care about me and my ideas, and (2) I can't believe it, you're not arguing with me or contradicting or belittling me or talking about your opinion of Bill. They'll think, "You didn't change the topic and go on to your own agenda. You accept me. I can be open, spontaneous, and frank with you."

Listen to a couple who don't communicate:

> *She:* How was the party last night?
> *He:* It was really great!
> *She:* Well, it's too bad you couldn't wait for me to go with you, but then thoughtfulness never was your strong suit.

If we could only get her to probe. How much more she would find out about him (even if she's been married to him for 30 years). Then she would be much more effective in her analyses and her subsequent decisions and actions with him. But she just had to jump in and try to influence (hurt) him. Why? Because she's afraid. No, you say, she's angry. But she's angry because she's afraid...afraid he's happy. Actually, she's probably angry because she's afraid he had a good time without her; she may feel insignificant to him, that he doesn't need her. If only she had continued her "interviewing." Then her proposed solutions to the problems of the relationship might fall right into place for her.

She: How was the party last night?
He: It was really great!
She: How so?

Good probing question. Now she'll be more likely to get a response from him that will provide her with useful information about him and their relationship, now and in the future.

They: The people who manage my apartment building really do a lousy job!
You: How so? (Instead of "That's nothing; you should see mine. You wouldn't believe what I have to put up with. Why, just the other day..." Focus on others!)

They: I think I need a change of scenery.
You: Because? (Instead of "You and me both?' Stop trying to please them; you don't even know yet if agreeing with them will.)

They: I like a small-town atmosphere.
You: Because? (Instead of "You're kidding. You'll be bored to death." Too judgmental.)

They: I think Marcia's a terrific person.
You: How so? (Instead of "Let me tell you how I see Marcia in a deep psychological sense.")

They: I thought that was the worst movie I've seen in five years.
You: Because? (Instead of, "I couldn't disagree more. Actually, it's my mother's favorite movie").

The Difficulty of Using Probes. Probes are the essence of good evaluating because they bring out spontaneous, open, and meaningful behavior. But probes are difficult to do. Why? Because we are driven by our own fears. Listening to someone else often triggers our own fears and leads to an overwhelming desire to influence, to change the other person and their views, and to get them to focus on and be impressed by us. But which will lead someone to respect, like, and seek us out more, showing them our brilliance or admiring theirs?

Using probes effectively will give us a more accurate picture of who a person is and where we want to be with them. It will make us more successful at influencing them later, if we so desire. And good questioning techniques (being nonjudgmental, asking broad, general questions, using probes) will lead others to like us more. And being liked by someone makes influencing them much easier.

Using a Gentle Tone of Voice

Too often, we just focus on the words we use in our attempts to influence others. A person's tone of voice is an unusually critical factor in personal interactions. Tone communicates virtually all our feelings. **Our tone is often far more important than words when we're trying to influence people.**

> *Enthusiastic:* That's a beautiful tie!
> *Questioning:* That's a beautiful tie?
> Same words—entirely different meaning.

> *With feeling:* You know I love you.
> *Questioning:* You know I love you?
> Same words—entirely different meaning.

Actions do not speak louder than words; words (and the tone of voice they are "played to") are actions, and their impact on people is enormous. It is illegal to yell "FIRE!" in a crowded theater or say the word "bomb" in an airport.

When we think of words, however, we should automatically think of tone of voice. Some studies suggest that words account for only about seven percent of the impact our communications have on others—ninety three percent of our influence on others (and theirs on us) is tone and facial and body gestures.

More than anything else, our tone conveys our enthusiasm, disappointment, desire, anger, frustrations, our hopes, and our fears. So more than anything else, our tone will determine our impact on people. (A useful exercise is to tape yourself talking to people. But instead of focusing on your hair or makeup, listen to your tone of voice. Is it inflected? Does it convey emotional responsiveness? If not, maybe some acting classes or speech courses that emphasize expressiveness might be in order.)

Tone for Evaluating Others. When we interact in our evaluative mode, our tone must be soft and gentle. It must convey concern, respect, and interest in the other person. Our tone must be inflected; it must have a wide range, often starting in the upper register and ending in the lower.

Try saying, "How do you like your company?" first in a flat monotone in a low register. Then say it with inflection, starting at an uncomfortably high note (almost falsetto), then descending to the lower register. A gentle, inflected (high, then low), interested, and respectful tone of voice is probably the most difficult part of good evaluative interactions for most people. This is especially true of males. Having seen too many John Wayne movies, many men can't help but ask questions in a low, flat, authoritative tone of voice, trying to show everyone how powerful and strong they are.

> *Commanding:* Tell me about your apartment!
> *Soft, gentle, inflected:* Could you tell me a little about your apartment?

> *Commanding:* Tell me about yourself!
> *Soft, inflected, interested, and respectful:* Could you tell me a little about yourself?

Too many of us approach evaluative interactions fearing what others think of us, rather than focusing on what we know and can learn about the other person. For example, individuals who are fearful of being seen as weak and frightened and who must present a macho image usually make poor interviewers and poor judges of people. In fact, they usually make poor partners. Why? Because fear drives too much of their behavior. It leads them to spend too much of their time trying to convince others that they are strong and brave and too little time focusing on the needs and feelings of those around them. This can prove disastrous, especially in a personal relationship.

The low, flat, authoritative tone of voice generally makes the other person guarded, defensive, and resentful. The gentle, inflected, respectful approach generally makes the other person comfortable, spontaneous, relaxed, happy, and open.

The proper inflection will, like probes, tell the other person that you care, that you're really concerned about them. And no one can help liking a person who cares about them! It'll put the person at ease. And that's what we want. Why? Because then they're more likely to be themselves—and that's also what we want. And, as an added benefit, they'll want to be with us. No one likes being with a person who makes them feel uncomfortable.

Letting the Other Person Lead

As we've seen, the person who asks the questions controls the interaction. However, responding to our questions may lead some people to grow uncomfortable and subconsciously feel that they are being controlled or even interrogated. We will blunt this feeling by asking broad, general questions in a soft tone of voice and by focusing our next question on some part of the person's last response.

We want the person to know that we are listening and that we are concerned with, and care about, them. If our next question relates to some element in their last response, they'll know we're listening and they'll be more inclined to feel they are controlling the interaction. By following their lead, as we've seen, we are also delving into an area they *want* to talk about or at least feel is safe.

Leading by Following. Suppose we're talking to a fellow at a party who recently moved to Chicago from St. Louis and just mentioned that fact. Good questions might be "How was St. Louis?" or "How do you like Chicago?" or "How would you compare Chicago to St. Louis?" (Then follow their perfunctory response with a probe).

Bad questions would be "What kind of car do you drive?" or "Have you seen any good movies lately?" or "What's your favorite TV show?" These questions tell the person we really don't care about them or what they are saying. They indicate that we have our own agenda to which they must subscribe. These unrelated questions unequivocally state that we do not want to focus on them nearly as much as we want them to focus on us and those things *we* find interesting.

By asking unrelated (non-sequitur) questions which have nothing to do with the other person's concerns, we are running the risk of increasing their fear. We may inadvertently delve into areas that are frightening to them. They might feel that we are unpredictable. They may dislike the topic we raised with our "new" question. Actually, the mere act of someone's asking an unrelated question not only frustrates people, it often scares them. It makes them feel that they are being controlled, or even dominated, just the opposite of what we want.

By asking questions of at least one element of their last response, we are allowing them to feel that they are in control. We are responding to their lead and to the behavior they display in response to our original broad question.

Worse than asking bad questions, but even more common, is expressing our own views without acknowledging theirs ("extinction"). This is especially true if we do so prematurely, i.e., before we know the person. This behavior on our part tells the person that we really don't care about them. It tells them we feel they should care about us and our views, not themselves. It tells them we want to be the center of attention and our thoughts are more important to us than theirs.

If You're Focused On Me, You Must Care. Nothing can get a person to care about us more than our caring about them, their thoughts, feelings, and opinions. And nothing will convey our caring attitude more effectively and forcefully than our asking them questions, using the five principles we've discussed.

We can always reject someone. We just need to make sure that they don't want to reject us before we even get to know them. Effective questioning and accurate interpretations will put us in that position.

Let's now look at more examples of good and bad interactions:

> *Them:* There was something about that movie I really liked.
> *Good (any probe) or:* Can you pinpoint what it was?
> *Bad:* Let me tell you about a movie I just saw.
> *Worse:* Don't you think the theater is more stimulating than movies?

> *Them:* Skiing is my one great escape.
> *Good (any probe) or:* Really? How do you feel when you're going down the slope?
> *Bad:* How about reading? Don't you like to curl up with some of the classics for intellectual stimulation?
> *Worse:* My favorite getaway is cooking; I could cook for hours. One of my favorite dishes is...

> *Them:* I just don't seem to get a kick out of my job anymore.
> *Good (any probe) or:* What seems to be missing?
> *Bad:* Don't you think most things get boring after awhile?
> *Worse:* I really enjoy my job. I have so many interesting...

> *Them:* I really look forward to moving there.

Good (any probe) or: What do you look forward to most?
Bad: Do you have all your packing done?
Worse: I'd miss all my friends here (or I hate moving).

Them: I really wanted to get out on my own.
Good (any probe) or: What excited you most about it?
Bad: Oh, were your parents pretty controlling?
Worse: I got out on my own at an early age too. I left home when I…

Let's look at a few minutes of a good evaluative conversation. We're at a party and find ourselves standing next to a guy we've never met. Our tone of voice, as always, is soft, inflected and gentle.

Us: Really crowded in here.
He: Seems so.
Us: Hi, I'm Mary.
He: Hi, I'm John.
Us: Do you live around here?
He: No, actually I live in the downtown area.
Us: Oh really. How is living there?
He: Good.
Us: How so?
He: Well, the parking's a bit of a problem, but I love the variety of restaurants and activities there.
Us: What kind of restaurants do you like?
He: Really any kind, but Italian mostly, I suppose.
Us: Because?
He (laughs): Probably because a good friend of mine owns an Italian restaurant and he gives me a price break now and again.
Us (laughing too): That always helps.
He: Yeah, but I also help out there once in a while.
Us: Gee, what do you do?

He: One night I was the maitre' d.
Us: Really? How was that?
He: Oh, it was great.
Us: How so?
He: I never met so many people in my life. I just had a ball. There must have been six tables that kept yelling for me to sit with them.
Us: Did you?
He: Yeah.
Us: How'd it go?
He: Actually, at the end of the night I sat with a group of about twelve people. We wound up singing until two in the morning. It was a blast. But enough of me. How about you?

This interaction should have helped us build some rapport with this person. More importantly, it should have allowed us to have initially seen this person as being enthusiastically positive, able to laugh at himself, and people oriented. Although it represents only a few minutes of interaction, we should already be deciding if this person's influence on us will be constructive, and whether or not we'll continue the interaction.

Summary of Drawing Out the Behavior of Others

Focusing on others by asking them questions is a highly effective tool for evaluating people. The purpose of asking questions of someone is to elicit their most "frequent, repetitive" behavior. This will show us who a person truly is and how they will influence our attitudes and our confidence if we choose to interact with them frequently.

However, evaluating others can be an emotionally difficult process. It requires us to be nonjudgmental and to temporarily suppress our need to influence people.

Broad, general questions, gently put, elicit spontaneous, meaningful behavior from people, allowing them the freedom to respond any way they want. Their response tells us what interests them. Asking general questions lets the person bring up areas they find "safe" in discussing, hence they are inclined to find us a "safe" person to talk to (and lessening the fear of people when they're with us, especially in the initial stages of a relationship, is **always** one of our main goals).

Probing often elicits the most spontaneous, hence richest behavior for us to interpret regarding who this person is, whether we want to be with them, what kind of influence they'll likely have on us and our confidence over the long term. Good probes (to be frequently used in any conversation with virtually any person at almost any time) also tells the person we care about them and their views. Probing frequently tells us how to best influence a person and whether or not we should even want to try to influence this person.

Focusing on others, if done correctly, is applicable to, and effective in, virtually any human interaction. It should be an integral part of our repertoire, one that is readily and frequently called forth. When we're worried about having nothing to say to someone new in our lives, when we're unsure of how we feel about a person, or when we don't know why we dread upcoming interactions with a person, we would do well to remember to focus on others—the answers we're looking for are often in the questions we ask them.

Chapter Eighteen

Why Feedback Is Important

Continuous feedback and adjustment are essential to the health of any long-term relationship; therefore, before we develop such a relationship, we must make certain that our potential partner is open to constructive criticism from others. Some people are not, which means they'll have difficulty making the adjustments necessary. Their sensitivities (fears) lead to rigid (excessive) behaviors that make them poor candidates as friends and significant others.

An attractive, outgoing bachelor, for example, who fears being controlled may be a poor candidate for an intimate relationship. His ability to accept feedback may well be extremely limited. We want to know as quickly as possible who such folks are so we can get away from them and their inflexibility. Attempting to develop a viable long-term relationship with this type of person is almost certain to lead to frustration and a loss of self-confidence.

To Help or To Hurt—Timing Is Everything

Some people may resist our "constructive" suggestions because we make them at the wrong time in the wrong way. Too often, we give people "feedback" at the worst possible time—when we're most motivated to do so. And that is frequently when the person has done something we don't like. They've frustrated us and we're angry. And our goal, when we're angry, is to hurt, not help—and we usually do hurt them and the relationship.

How motivated is someone to tell her date that he has bad breath when he's just told her how radiant she looks? How motivated is someone to make this comment when he's just told her that her dress looks like something out of the fifties?

The best time to give constructive feedback is when everything is going well. Then our motivation is not to hurt, but to help—to constructively change the person. And the goal of any feedback is, or should be, to change someone for the better. What other goal could we possibly have in giving feedback?

When everything is going well, we are more likely to be calm, gently caring, and concerned in all our gestures, including that all-important tone of voice. Then the likelihood of altercation, anger, and hurt is minimal and the likelihood of constructive change is high.

Preventing Feedback

Some people, however, go to great lengths to avoid any feedback or suggestions from others, even to the point of attacking others. Hostile, frequently critical individuals try to prevent criticism directed at them by intimidating others, often using ridicule or criticism of others as the weapon. Others *passively* withdraw from people. These highly sensitive folks just run from people, especially open, blunt, and direct people.

It's the old "fight or flight" dichotomy. Both approaches, however, have the same goal—to prevent feedback, especially criticism. But fear of being criticized leads to excessive behavior, in this case either overly aggressive or overly passive.

The Necessity of Continuous Feedback

Both types of people, if successful in avoiding feedback, wind up functioning in a "vacuum." But any "closed" system always moves toward disorder (the law of entropy). Anyone who chokes off feedback, therefore, becomes a closed system, moving toward disorder.

This is not merely a theoretical construct. Feedback from others is our only check on reality. Left completely to our own devices, we would all end up in dreamland, in a state of disorder. The passive person who always withdraws from people and their feedback (flight) is the one who sometimes winds up in the clock tower, shooting people at random—always described as a nice guy, but "quiet and a loner" (i.e., a closed system). A "cult," before committing mass suicide, almost always cuts off communication with the "outside" world (i.e., it becomes a closed system).

The intimidator, on the other hand, is aggressive with everyone, and friends with no one. If the intimidator happens to head a company, he'll quickly drive it downhill. Because everyone fears eliciting his criticism, they'll be terrorized over giving him theirs. As a result, all decisions will rest on his shoulders and, without feedback from others, these decisions will often be poor ones.

If the intimidator happens to head a country, he'll also quickly drive it downhill. Most dictatorships fail because no one dares to give the "leader" any feedback. Consider someone telling Stalin what his greatest shortcoming was in running the country.

For both the excessively passive and the excessively aggressive person, functioning in a vacuum can lead to disastrous results, **especially for people around them.** We don't want that to be us.

Evaluating the Reaction to Criticism

We must try to determine how our potential life partner will respond to feedback, to the suggestions of other people. And we'll do so by saying and asking the question that follows in an informal, "spontaneous" setting when we are alone with them and everything is going quite well. We may even be talking pleasantly about something totally unrelated. We'll wait for a slight pause in the conversation. Then, remembering our tone of voice for good "interviewing," we'll make the following statement and ask the following question in the most gentle, caring, and concerned manner possible:

The Question: "You know, John, I feel that you might tend to be a little too sensitive to criticism at times. How do you feel about that?"

Notice the "wishy-washy" language used, phrases such as "might tend to be," "a little too," and "at times." We're really trying to be as nice as possible about this. We know that criticism given as a whisper is often heard as a shout. That's why criticism always should be given this way—in a gentle, casual manner.

If, on the other hand, we use this invaluable assessment tool (pointing our someone's sensitivity to criticism) when we are angry, we are more likely to say something like, "You are absolutely the most sensitive person I've ever met. I can't even breathe without your complaining about something! When are you going to grow up and get a life?" (This diatribe is justified, of course, as our way of "helping" them grow personally.)

The response to these criticisms may indicate to us how the person handles being attacked, but little else. And we don't care if we know how they handle being attacked because we certainly don't intend to have a long-term relationship with anyone if it involves a lot of fighting. Besides, their reaction probably wouldn't matter anyway. If they stayed with us after this type of personal attack (especially if it happened several times), we shouldn't want them around.

A Difficult Goal

Even gently put, this would be a difficult thing for some of us to say, especially to a significant other (try it on a good friend first). A moment of thought as to why it's difficult may well be in order. Is it difficult because the person we're speaking to is so sensitive? This is valuable knowledge. Can such a sensitive person make the small but frequent adjustments necessary in any long-term relationship? Will they respond constructively to even minor suggestions as to how a small change in their behavior could help the relationship? Or do we find it difficult to say this to someone because of our own uneasiness in the area of offering others feedback, constructive suggestions? If so, we have a little more work to do.

If we're unable to give those around us this "gentle" suggestion and feedback, we're putting them in a "vacuum," in a situation where they have to function in a fog with minimal guidance. Thus, we're doing them a grave disservice. After all, who is better positioned to give constructive suggestions to someone than a person who cares about them and knows them well? Thus, our sensitivities (fears) and inhibitions over giving criticism to others most hurt those we like. No one can help someone if they cannot offer constructive suggestions.

Our Goal

What is our goal here and now, when we're gently suggesting to someone that they're a little too sensitive to criticism at times? Our goal is not reaching some consensus with them, nor is it winning some argument. Our goal is to evaluate the person so we know what we're getting into with them over the long term.

Implicit in our gentle suggestion of their sensitivity to criticism is…a criticism. We are actually adopting both a content and a behavioral approach. With the content approach, we are saying they are too sensitive to criticism. Behaviorally, we are actually criticizing them. How they respond to our gentle feedback will tell us a great deal about our future (or lack of it) with this person.

The Reactions

We can, of course, boil people's responses down to two general reactions: agreement or disagreement. And we have learned that we can evaluate a response in one of two ways, through content or behavior. But we'll always rely on a behavioral, not a content, interpretation when we're looking at the person. (The fact is, of course, that we're all too sensitive to criticism.)

> *Agreement:* "You're probably right," John says. "I think I am a little too sensitive to criticism at times."
>
> *Content interpretation:* John is too sensitive to criticism (after all, he just said so). He will not, therefore, be amenable to suggestions from others. We need someone who will listen to others, so we should have doubts about John.
>
> *Behavioral interpretation:* John listens, respects and responds constructively and honestly to criticism and is, therefore, amenable to the suggestions of others. We should probably continue the relationship. John seems to be flexible and able to face reality.
>
> *Disagreement:* "No, I think you're wrong," John declares. "I don't think I'm too sensitive to criticism at all. Give me an example of when I was."
>
> *Content interpretation:* John must respond well to the suggestions of others because he's not sensitive to criticism. How do we know he's not sensitive to criticism? He just said so, hence that's an accurate content interpretation.
>
> *Behavioral interpretation:* John responds defensively to criticism, even criticism gently put. How do we know? He just did behaviorally. We might wish to reconsider a long-term relationship with him because of his apparent resistance to outside suggestions.

Watch the behavior, not the content! Who a person is behaviorally will be what you get over the long term. If the person is always intent on

impressing everyone, that's what you'll get: someone who is always trying to impress people. The content of what they say to impress people
may change frequently, but the behavior rarely does. Content is relatively easy to change; behavioral patterns are not.

It is the behavior of the person that will have an impact on you, that
will increase or decrease your love of people and yourself, your confidence or your fear. It is the behavior of the people in your inner circle,
whether or not they reinforce or punish or extinguish you and what
you're doing when they do these things that will influence what life is
and can be to you.

Confirmation

One other statement you might later use to check on how this person responds to outside feedback is to gently say, "I feel that at times
you might care a little too much about what others think of you. How
do you feel about that?"

Each of us may fear different things in people, but virtually all our
fears center on the behavior of others. That behavior is often
determined by what others think of us. Consequently, everyone cares
too much what others think of them; its the universal fear. If the person
agrees, they're amenable to outside suggestions. If they disagree, they're
probably not; they're denying reality.

Manipulation

Are we being too manipulative in these exercises? It depends on
your definition. Each time we say words, we're trying to influence
someone. We may do it well or we may do it poorly. But we're always
trying to do it. Doing it well is better. And we're most likely to do it
well if we think, and use good sense and do an accurate evaluation of
a person. Thus, "knowing" what we are doing, rather than merely

responding spontaneously to the dictates of our feelings, is probably in the best interest of everyone.

Summary

To build a compatible long-term relationship requires periodic adjustments by both parties. Knowing how amenable this potential life partner is to feedback and suggestions from others is, therefore, quite important.

One way to determine that is to gently suggest, when everything is going well, that they "tend to be a little too sensitive to criticism at times."

All constructive feedback like this should be immediately followed by eliciting a reaction from them. Therefore, the question "How do you feel about that?" should be asked immediately.

If the person disagrees and denies sensitivity to criticism, they're highly sensitive to criticism and probably resistant to the input of others. Their rigidity and resistance to change will likely make them poor life partners.

If the person agrees to being too sensitive to criticism, they are accepting reality and are probably amenable to outside influences. They are more likely to be flexible and should be considered further for the crucial "significant other" position in our lives.

Epilogue

Karen is a 40 year old, twice divorced, quite attractive woman. As with most people, Karen has been more successful in her professional carrer than in her personal life. Both her ex-husbands were verbally abusive. She had seriously dated two other men, each of whom was married at the time (and remained married, promises to the contrary). She presently lives with a 56 year old math teacher who has told her, without hesitation, that he will never marry.

Karen has worked for the past year at a "not for profit" organization. She has stayed there because she considers her boss, Larry, to be one of the best she's ever had, a compassionate man. She's also personally attracted to him because he's married, has three children, and is as unavailable as her math teacher.

On her one year anniversary at the job, Larry took Karen out for drinks, as he does with every employee. Karen had two glasses of wine, which proved to be one too many. She made a pass at Larry which he gently, but firmly, rejected. This depressed her to the point of having a third glass of wine while unburdening herself.

Larry: Karen, if I may say so, you seem to be choosing the wrong people to fall in love with.

Karen: No kidding. What a startling revelation.

Larry: Well, I think it's important to acknowledge and talk about. I feel that the people I have to deal with have an enormous influence on me, an influence I don't think I'm often aware of.

Karen: You're trying to tell me that I bring the wrong people into my life. I'm aware of all that. Why do I do it? Worse, why do I then do so many dumb things to keep them in my life? Look at the guy I'm presently living with. I should have left him months ago.

Larry: You know, before coming here, I was in a really tough, competitive company and I had a guy working for me who was awfully indecisive. Everyone told me to fire him. And I really wanted to, but I just couldn't bring myself to do it. I talked to him about it, but that only affected him for a day or two. Believe me, he had to be aware of my frustration, my anger over his indecisiveness.

Karen: Did he ever change?

Larry: Yeah, the more I talked to him about it, the worse he got. And that was a problem because, as his supervisor, I was responsible for him.

Karen: Why didn't you just fire him?

Larry: Probably for the same reason you can't get crummy people out of your life.

Karen: Touche.

Larry: I've always had a problem doing that, even when I know it's the right thing to do. Anyway, at the time, I was getting anxious because my boss was starting to wonder about me.

Karen: What happened?

Larry: One day I tried to picture what the perfect employee in that job would be like. Then I asked myself why this guy wasn't being the perfect employee. And this led me down a whole new track, one that actually worked pretty well.

Karen: How so?

Larry: Well, I had been focused on what he was doing wrong, on his indecisiveness. That would frustrate me and I'd get angry. Then I'd yell at him for being indecisive. But then it dawned on me that I was making him more fearful. And this made him even more indecisive.

Karen: What'd you do?

Larry: Instead of focusing on why he was bad, I started to think about why he couldn't be good. Instead of focusing on why he was indecisive, I started to ask myself why he wasn't decisive.

Karen: And?

Larry: And I realized he was afraid of being decisive. So I began focusing on his fear of being decisive rather than his frustrating indecisiveness.

Karen: And?

Larry: I concluded he wasn't decisive because he was always afraid of being criticized. And boy, was he. So I began to work with him on that.

Karen: How so?

Larry: I made him ask people in the company what his greatest shortcoming was.

Karen: He must have loved that.

Larry: No, but desperate times call for desperate measures. And I was getting desperate because the people who said I should fire him started wondering about firing me. Actually, I told him if he didn't ask people about his shortcomings, I was going to fire him.

Karen: That's a sobering association; do what I say or you're out. What happened?

Larry: To my surprise, it kind of worked. A lot of the people who were complaining about him and wanted me to fire him had an opportunity to complain directly to him. This took some of the pressure off me. Then he seemed to get less sensitive to criticism. I guess getting so much of it desensitized him to it. And people seemed to like him more, probably because they were able to tell him what they really thought. Eventually he did become more decisive and even got promoted...over me.

Karen: That must have done wonders for your ego.

Larry: I was ticked at first. But I wanted to leave that company anyway. Besides, he was always very appreciative for what I had done for him. He'd get quite emotional thanking me. I guess that went a long way with me.

Karen: What does all this have to do with me?

Larry: I wonder if we're focusing on the wrong things when we have problems. When I see a problem with someone now, I don't ask myself what he's doing wrong and what I can do to stop him from doing it wrong. Instead, I try to picture what he should be doing right and why he can't. And it's usually fear that keeps him from doing the right thing. What we do wrong isn't the key; what we can't do right is.

Karen: How would you apply that to my life?

Larry: You've been focused on why you like men who are bad for you. Then you berate yourself, lose more confidence and keep doing whatever it is you're doing to trap yourself with the wrong kind of guy.

I think you should focus on why you fear men who are good for you. THAT'S the problem. When you answer that question, you might actually start doing the right thing.

Karen: All right, why do I?

Larry: I don't know. But try to picture the ideal woman in your mind and ask yourself why you're not that. What part of being ideal do you fear?

Actually, I think, and this is just an amateur talking, that you fear intimacy with men. You're choosing men who also fear intimacy. You feel safe with them because they don't confront your fear. But don't focus on that. Focus on why you fear being with men who are confident enough to like intimacy.

Karen: There aren't many of them around.

Larry: Maybe not. But there are a few, and I'm sure you've met some of them. And I'm just as sure you found something wrong with them.

Karen: They're probably boring. That's not a novel phenomenon among men, you know.

Larry: If you fear something, it's easy to find reasons to get away from it.

Karen: What would you suggest I do?

Larry: You've got to get yourself to like intimacy if that's the problem. Maybe you fear intimacy because you associate it with rejection. Maybe when you had an intimate relationship, you got rejected. Even parents can do that to us.

But the point is, you've got to deliberately and consciously want the thing you fear, the behavior in others you fear. And because you want it, you'll seek it out, experience it, and maybe find it isn't so scary after all. But that means looking to be with people who are comfortable with intimacy.

Karen: Easier said than done.

Larry: No question. But remember, it isn't that you like men who fear intimacy. It's that you fear men who are comfortable with intimacy. That's why you'll probably stay the way you are. You're avoiding the people who would help you most.

Karen: How motivating you are. You want me to love my enemies.

Larry: At least interact with them. Some of them anyway. But you'll need help doing it. Someone in your life who can prod you to find people who are comfortable with intimacy, and curse you when you run away from them.

Karen: How about you?

Larry: No way. Karen, you're a very attractive woman. But I'm afraid helping you in that area would get me into things better left to others.

Karen: Now who's being afraid of intimacy?

Larry: But in some situations, that's good. And this is one of them.

Karen: I can't be afraid of intimacy, but you can be. Aren't we being a little hypocritical?

Larry: I don't think so. Almost everything we do is appropriate sometimes and not appropriate sometimes. The confident person knows which is which and can act accordingly. They have much more flexibility than the person driven by fear.

Karen: So you're confident with intimacy because you're flexible now and you feel rejecting an intimate relationship with me is appropriate. Isn't that a little self-serving?

Larry: Probably. But I think this just happens to be an area I'm confident in. I have a great family that makes me pretty comfortable with intimacy. But believe me, there are plenty of areas I'm not comfortable with.

Karen: Such as?

Larry (laughs): Firing incompetent people when I should. But you raise a good point. The only one who can help you is someone who is confident in the area you're looking at. Our problem is we pick as friends people who share our fears. And they can't help us. Worse, we avoid those who don't share our fears because they might confront us. That's why we don't change.

Karen: You think my friends are my real enemies.

Larry: At least watch the influence your friends have on you. I'm too cautious. And you'll notice my friends are almost always cautious. And because of that, they're not likely to help me become more risk oriented. Quite the opposite.

You've probably always picked men who share your fear of being intimate. They can't help you overcome that fear. Actually they don't want to. You have to want men in your life who like intimacy or at least are comfortable with it. You don't have to date them. Just have them around.

If you want to change yourself, sometimes you have to get new friends.